Feeding Jesus Sheep

10 TIMELESS TRUTHS FOR GODLY SERVICE

MARCIA FURROW

 World Publishing and Productions

Feeding Jesus' Sheep: 10 Timeless Principles for Godly Service

Copyright ©2026 Marcia Furrow

Published by World Publishing and Productions, PO Box 8722, Jupiter, FL 33468
Worldpublishingandproductions.com

All rights reserved. This book is protected under the copyright laws of the United States of America. No portion of this book may be reproduced, distributed, or transmitted in any form, including photocopying, recording, or other electronic or mechanical methods, without the written permission of the publisher, excepted in the case of brief quotations embodied in reviews and certain other non-commercial uses permitted by copyright law.

ISBN: 978-1-957111-59-9

Library of Congress Control Number: 2026905370

Unmarked Scripture quotations are taken from the ESV® Bible (The Holy Bible, English Standard Version®), © 2001 by Crossway, a publishing ministry of Good News Publishers. Used by permis-sion. All rights reserved.

Scripture quotations marked NIV are taken from THE HOLY BIBLE, NEW INTERNATIONAL VERSION®, NIV® Copyright © 1973, 1978, 1984, 2011 by Biblica, Inc.® Used by permission. All rights reserved worldwide.

To Brian —
Your servant heart is a role model for me.

To Dan and Nikki, Bob and Jen, Jake, Matt,
Cal, Stella, JoJo, Bennett, and Wyatt —
It is my privilege to have the honor of serving you.

Contents

Acknowledgments	VII
Foreword	IX
Introduction	XI
The Gospel Versions of the Miracle of Feeding the Five Thousand	XV
1. Servants Lead; Leaders Serve	1
2. Begin with Jesus	9
3. Hone Your Vision	29
4. Expect Tests	49
5. Nothing Is Too Wonderful for God	67
6. What God Requires, God Provides	87
7. There Is No Confusion in God	109
8. Pray Continually	125
9. Dependent Distributors	143
10. Acknowledge Needs	161
11. Surrender	177
12. It Is Impossible to Expend the Eternal	191
Afterword	199

Acknowledgments

This book is the product of many years of training, which I had both the privilege of receiving and the responsibility of giving. I want to thank Bible Study Fellowship for providing such excellent institute trainings with the most notable and wise theologians.

I also want to thank the leaders who have sat under my training. Iron does indeed sharpen iron, and I would not be the servant I am today if you had not challenged and encouraged me.

To Lynn Davis, Brian Furrow, Ketra Hancock, Christa March, Derek Mason, Anita McGinnis, and the late Jane Roach, thank you for reading and critiquing the initial manuscript and providing feedback and encouragement. Your love, time, and expertise are appreciated more than you know. You are truly servants of the Most High God.

To the staff at World Publishing and Productions—Julie, Kimberly, and Kelly, God has surely used your servant hearts to minister to me. Without you, this book would still be a work in progress.

Foreword

As Christ followers, we encounter individuals who stand out as "good leaders" and those who embody the qualities of a "godly leader." Marcia Furrow is a shining example of the latter. With her vast experience as a Bible study leader, God has used her to feed many of Jesus' sheep. And she has done so with grace and godly wisdom.

I have been blessed to pray alongside Marcia and witness firsthand how God has worked through her life and in this, her latest book. *Feeding Jesus' Sheep* is more than just another leadership book; it delves into the profound questions and concerns Christian leaders face daily. By reflecting on the miraculous feeding of the five thousand, Marcia beautifully reminds us that while Jesus *commands* us to care for his flock as his twelve disciples did, we must first allow him to train us. This training equips us to learn—and ultimately guide others—to feed Jesus' sheep.

I encourage you to read this book that has profoundly impacted my own understanding of what it means to be a godly leader.

Thank you, Marcia, for your obedience to Jesus Christ in writing this book. He is the greatest teacher.

-*Christa March*
CEO, Teen Mother Choices

Introduction

"Rapidly" barely describes how quickly things are changing in the church, yet one thing remains constant: Jesus' people need tending to. They are hungry and hurting, and they require care to get or stay healthy. So many are crying out for someone to serve them, yearning for ordinary people like you and me who love Jesus and his flock to nurture them. Now more than ever, the church needs godly servants to step up and take our God-ordained places as the servants Jesus has called and commissioned us to be.

Before ascending to the Father, Jesus told Peter, an ordinary fisherman, to feed his sheep (John 21:15-18), and Peter did for the rest of his life. And Jesus' apostles, the Twelve, also did. Now, it is our turn. And the sheep are hungry! Yet, to accomplish the task effectively—without giving up, burning out, or falling short—we must be equipped. Just as Jesus prepared Peter for his calling, he is teaching and empowering us for ours today. In this book, we will examine ten principles Jesus used as he physically fed more than five thousand hungry seekers while training the Twelve to feed people spiritually. These timeless principles enable you and me to serve and lead others effectively today—whether we are brand-new believers or seasoned saints.

What does it look like to step out in faith and tend to Jesus' sheep? How do we overcome the fear of leading a flock into the wrong pasture? How do we defeat the paralysis brought about by a worry of inadequacy so that we can dance in victory? How do we serve when we feel *we* are in need of being served?

Feeding Jesus' Sheep identifies ten principles that guide us to become godly servants as we follow our calling, despite our insufficiencies, trusting in our wonderfully sufficient Savior. These principles will remind us that Jesus will never let us down; he will always enable us to follow him where he leads.

As you read and partner with Jesus, know he will equip and elevate you as his servant, filling you with the Holy Spirit and empowering you to efficiently and effectively feed his sheep as you point them toward him, our one and only Savior. Through Jesus' training and the power of the Holy Spirit, you will learn how to overcome anything that threatens to lead you to starvation, frustration, or burnout.

God will bless and empower you as you witness Jesus train the Twelve, and you will develop a new understanding that Jesus' own apostles were as incapable of feeding the multitudes on that hillside so many years ago as we are today. Despite their deficiencies, Jesus invited the Twelve into the difficult—the impossible, really—and used every moment, every circumstance, and every detail to train them to serve efficiently and effectively. Jesus also invites you and me into the difficulties and impossibilities of events today, and he will teach us as we step into the shoes (well, sandals) of the Twelve.

On that day, Jesus not only physically fed the five thousand men (plus all of the women and children) but also physically and spiritually fed the Twelve. What Jesus taught that day prepared the Twelve to serve for a lifetime without going hungry, giving up, or burning out. What he wanted for them then, he also wants for us today. Our mighty God is calling you to serve well, without reservation and with exuberant joy.

As we work, verse by verse, through the miracle of feeding the five thousand, we will see our Master Teacher at work. We will hear his words to the Twelve and understand what it means to rely on Jesus to get the job done without exhausting ourselves or our resources. As we learn and put these ten principles into practice, identifying with and leaning on Jesus, we will see our abilities and confidence grow proportionally as we witness his miraculous power at work in us.

Wherever you are in your service or leadership experience, this book will encourage you and remind you that God has a path of service he has specifically prepared for you, and he will see you through triumphantly.

This book is not a formula or a set of steps that will magically equip you to become a godly leader. Instead, it is a set of principles that teaches how to be godly and practical servants in the kingdom of God by primarily focusing on the why: Jesus. We are not alone as we serve the Lord and his people. Instead, we are the sacred go-betweens called to feed Jesus' sheep and care for his lambs. As we more fully understand the reality and limitations of our role and the truth and the limitlessness of Jesus' person and position, godly service will become natural.

If you are a new Christian debating whether you can take on a service responsibility, remember that the Twelve had the same questions and concerns.

If you are in the thick of serving and are craving a shot of adrenaline to keep up the good fight, get ready to be infused.

If you are a seasoned veteran of Christian service who has nothing left to give and is questioning whether to stop or continue plugging away out of obligation, this book will help you find the answer.

If you desire to serve but wonder where you will find the time, energy, desire, love, passion, and compassion to do what seems impossible, remember, the Twelve wondered, too.

If you are facing a difficult task, questioning whether you can succeed; if failure seems inevitable barring a miracle, and, in all honesty, you aren't even sure what success looks like, remember that the Twelve faced the same overwhelming dilemma.

If you have been excusing yourself from the call to serve because you're too busy, too frightened, too apprehensive, too young, too old, or you're not even sure of the call, remember that Jesus has heard those same excuses since he walked on earth in the flesh. And yet, though he has heard it all, our Lord and Savior still loves and uses even the most hesitant believers.

You are not alone in your hesitations, but know that Jesus is with you and has positioned you for a remarkable season you cannot yet imagine. Our faithful and creative God is all about making godly servants, and nothing is more exciting, challenging, or fulfilling than following his call. You are in for a beautiful ride. Buckle up!

The Gospel Versions of the Miracle of Feeding the Five Thousand

There is a reason the Holy Spirit inspired the telling of Jesus feeding the five thousand, a remarkable moment in history, in all four Gospels: This astounding miracle immediately impacted thousands and continues to affect believers thousands of years later. While most of us are likely familiar with this Bible story, before we dive into all it has for us, let us take a moment to refresh ourselves on the details of Scripture by reading the actual words of God.

Matthew 14:13-22

Now when Jesus heard this, he withdrew from there in a boat to a desolate place by himself. But when the crowds heard it, they followed him on foot from the towns. When he went ashore he saw a great crowd, and he had compassion on them and healed their sick. Now when it was evening, the disciples came to him and said, "This is a desolate place, and the day is now over; send the crowds away to go into the villages and buy food for themselves." But Jesus said, "They need not go away; you give them something to eat." They said to him, "We have only five loaves here and two fish." And he said, "Bring them here to me." Then he ordered the crowds to sit down on the grass, and taking the five loaves and the two fish, he looked up to heaven and said a blessing. Then he broke the loaves and gave them to the disciples, and the disciples gave them to the crowds. And they all ate and were satisfied. And they took up twelve baskets full of the broken pieces left over. And those who ate were about five thousand men, besides women and children.

Mark 6:30-44

The apostles returned to Jesus and told him all that they had done and taught. And he said to them, "Come away by yourselves to a desolate place and rest a while." For many were coming and going, and they had no leisure even to eat. And they went away in the boat to a desolate place by themselves. Now many saw them going and recognized them, and they ran there on foot from all the towns and got there ahead of them. When he went ashore he saw a great crowd, and he had compassion on them, because they were like sheep without a shepherd. And he began to teach them many things. And when it grew late, his disciples came to him and said, "This is a desolate place, and the hour is now late. Send them away to go into the surrounding countryside and villages and buy themselves something to eat." But he answered them, "You give them something to eat." And they said to him, "Shall we go and buy two hundred denarii worth of bread and give it to them to eat?" And he said to them, "How many loaves do you have? Go and see." And when they had found out, they said, "Five, and two fish." Then he commanded them all to sit down in groups on the green grass. So they sat down in groups, by hundreds and by fifties. And taking the five loaves and the two fish, he looked up to heaven and said a blessing and broke the loaves and gave them to the disciples to set before the people. And he divided the two fish among them all. And they all ate and were satisfied. And they took up twelve baskets full of broken pieces and of the fish. And those who ate the loaves were five thousand men.

Luke 9:10–17

On their return the apostles told him all that they had done. And he took them and withdrew apart to a town called Bethsaida. When the crowds learned it, they followed him, and he welcomed them and spoke to them of the kingdom of God and cured those who had need of healing. Now the day began to wear away, and the twelve came and said to him, "Send the crowd away to go into the surrounding villages and countryside to find lodging and get provisions, for we are here in a desolate place." But he said to them, "You give them something to eat." They said, "We have no more than five loaves and two fish—unless we are to go and buy food for all these people." For there were about five thousand men. And he said to his disciples, "Have them sit down in groups of about fifty each." And they did so, and had them all sit down. And taking the five loaves and the two fish, he looked up to heaven and said a blessing over them. Then he broke the loaves and gave them to the disciples to set before the crowd. And they all ate and were satisfied. And what was left over was picked up, twelve baskets of broken pieces.

John 6:1-15

After this Jesus went away to the other side of the Sea of Galilee, which is the Sea of Tiberias. And a large crowd was following him, because they saw the signs that he was doing on the sick. Jesus went up on the mountain, and there he sat down with his disciples. Now the Passover, the feast of the Jews, was at hand. Lifting up his eyes, then, and seeing that a large crowd was coming toward him, Jesus said to Philip, "Where are we to buy bread, so that these people may eat?" He said this to test him, for he himself knew what he would do. Philip answered him, "Two hundred denarii worth of bread would not be enough for each of them to get a little." One of his disciples, Andrew, Simon Peter's brother, said to him, "There is a boy here who has five barley loaves and two fish, but what are they for so many?" Jesus said, "Have the people sit down." Now there was much grass in the place. So the men sat down, about five thousand in number. Jesus then took the loaves, and when he had given thanks, he distributed them to those who were seated. So also the fish, as much as they wanted. And when they had eaten their fill, he told his disciples, "Gather up the leftover fragments, that nothing may be lost." So they gathered them up and filled twelve baskets with fragments from the five barley loaves left by those who had eaten. When the people saw the sign that he had done, they said, "This is indeed the Prophet who is to come into the world!"

Perceiving then that they were about to come and take him by force to make him king, Jesus withdrew again to the mountain by himself.

Chapter 1
Servants Lead; Leaders Serve

*So neither he who plants nor he who waters
is anything, but only God who gives the growth.
1 Corinthians 3:7*

Why did you pick up this book? Let me guess. You are reading this book because you are either currently serving or considering serving in your church or another Christian organization and want to get it right. Understanding the difference between good and godly, you want to be more than a good servant; you want to be a godly servant—to fulfill the role God has planned for you in the best possible way. Your passion to serve for God's glory requires more than just doing something well; it requires the same mindset and heart attitude of those you admire, those who lead you. You want to be like them: a godly leader.

Perhaps you are thinking, "I just want to be a servant, a godly servant. Does that mean I have to *lead*?" Well, yes, because when you are serving, you are leading. Leading for Christ doesn't always come with a title. You may not be in the pulpit, a worship leader, a deacon, an elder, or a teacher—or maybe you do hold one of those positions, but you still don't think of yourself as a leader.

Leading? Yikes! For some of us, that is a scary thought. We might see ourselves as servants, but leaders? Now that's a different ballgame; leaders are the people others follow. Exactly. And, those you have the privilege to serve—whether in the nursery or the kitchen, through committees that work behind the scenes, in Sunday School, or through teaching and training—are following your lead, either toward Jesus or away from him. There are only two paths. Because you have a heart to serve others and have picked up this book, it is evident that you want to lead people to Jesus. You want to be a godly servant in whatever capacity God has for you. That makes you a leader.

It is important to clarify from the start that just as Jesus *came not to be served, but to serve* (Matthew 20:28), so too, we, as members of our church communities, must not come merely as consumers or as those desiring to be served, but as family members willing to help. We can all agree that Jesus was more than a servant; he was a leader. In fact, Jesus was and is the ultimate leader. People followed him in droves when he walked on this earth, and people still do. And they will follow you as you represent him and serve his people.

Therefore, it is safe to say that leaders serve by leading and servants lead by serving; that's how the church operates. So, we will be using service and leadership interchangeably throughout this book. Godly leaders are servants, and godly servants are leaders. Whether you have recognized that in the past or not, now you know. God has commissioned you to both serve and lead.

Since you are still reading this book and want to be the godliest servant you can be, the foremost questions are: Is there a difference between a good leader and a godly leader? What, then, is a good leader? And, how do you become a godly servant who leads?

We all know what good leaders look like: they're reliable, trustworthy, compassionate, knowledgeable, responsible, and personable. We could name many more attributes of good leaders, and you probably possess most of them. But what makes a *godly* leader? The Bible provides the answer. When Jesus fed the five thousand, he revealed ten leadership principles that godly leaders possess. You may recognize some of these characteristics; you may even feel that some may define you. But there will likely be others that will feel foreign.

Can you be or become a godly leader? Yes. How do you do it? I'm glad you asked! As you continue reading, take time to process and lean in to these ten principles gleaned directly from God's Word.

Let's begin with an overview. Godly leaders have and practice the following:

- **Jesus.** Godly servants start with Jesus. We come to Jesus first for salvation, and then he begins the work of sanctification in us (gradually growing us individually into a person who looks and acts like Jesus). As godly servants, we don't just know *about* Jesus; we are in a relationship *with* him. He knows us, and we know him.

- **Vision.** Godly servants want to see as Jesus sees. Our focus is not on ourselves but on others; we strive to see people and things from Jesus' perspective, looking beyond what is visible to see and perceive the invisible.

- **Tests.** Godly servants embrace the hard things—the trials—knowing that it is often in the test that God reveals our faith. We welcome God's training and pruning, which can come through difficult, if not humanly impossible, circumstances.

- **Calling.** Godly servants know their service is more than a choice; it is a calling from God, and it fully aligns with their gifting and personality. We know that when we are called into a place of service, we have a front-row seat to watch God at work in the lives of those he has called us to serve.

- **Trust.** Godly servants know that God provides exactly what we need to do what he asks of us. We do not have to trust in our limited resources, strength, or ability because God is limitless in his resources, strength, and ability, and he will see to it that all our needs are met.

- **God's Will.** Godly servants know that God has a plan for their service, and he will accomplish that plan. We know God uses our circumstances, the truth of his Word, and the inner peace of obedience to reveal his will to us, and we choose to follow his way with confidence.

- **Prayer.** Godly servants have an open line of communication with God and use it often. We trust that God knows what is happening in our lives and what is best for us; still, we ask for what we need and we practice gratitude in all circumstances.

- **Defined Roles.** Godly servants know that they ultimately serve God. We do everything as unto the Lord and are amazed when he does spectacular things through us. We know who we are and who we are not, and we willingly let God be God in all things.

- **Satisfaction.** Godly servants are satisfied in the Lord despite our circumstances. We know that God is sufficient, and we choose to rest in him.

- **Submission.** Godly servants know they are ultimately soldiers. We fight under the headship of the King of kings and the Lord of lords and submit to him in every realm.

You may think you don't sufficiently possess or regularly practice these ten attributes of a godly servant, but don't worry; that's the book's purpose: to describe and expound on these principles so that they will become second nature to you and help you become the godly servant both you and God desire you to be. Nevertheless, I must stress that this book is not a formula nor a list of things to do. Instead, it identifies what our attitude and motivation will be when we allow the Holy Spirit to work in us, empowering us to serve God's greater purpose. We cannot muster up the oomph to do and be what we have been called to without God's presence and power. Striving to be more than good is too exhausting when we rely solely on our own strength. Therefore, our primary motivation and power for service must be found in God. God—his purpose, plans, and glory—must be preeminent in whatever we do for his church. We want to be godly servants. That is our goal. Will we succeed? I think so! How can we not when that is also God's goal for us?

Godly servants give glory to God first and foremost and have a mindset that God is the reason for and the goal of our leadership.

Oh, the depth of the riches and wisdom and knowledge of God! How unsearchable are his judgments and how inscrutable his ways! "For who has known the mind of the Lord, or who has been his counselor?" "Or who has given a gift to him that he might be repaid?" For from him and through him and to him are all things. To him be glory forever. Amen (Romans 11:33-36).

We cannot add to God, and we cannot take away from God. We don't serve in order to advance ourselves, our reputations, our glory, or our agenda; we serve because we love the Lord and, by extension, we love his people. We are blessed to serve his people and challenged to be more than good servants; we will be godly servants.

Oswald Chambers wrote, "The questions that truly matter in life are remarkably few, and they are all answered by these words— 'Come to Me.' Our Lord's words are not, 'Do this, or don't do that,' but— 'Come to me.' If I will simply come to Jesus, my real life will be brought into harmony with my real desires."[1] If my real desire is to serve God by being a godly servant, I must begin by coming to Jesus.

This book will help us gain a new understanding of what it means to become what we desire: a godly servant of the Lord Jesus Christ. We will also learn through these ten principles that to succeed, we must come to Jesus first so that we might persevere in him.

If we desire to feed Jesus' sheep without starving ourselves—without giving up or giving out—we must come to Jesus before we do anything else. What do I mean by "come to Jesus"? Simply, as a response to his love for us and our love for him, we commit our hearts, our souls, our minds, and our will to him. As we do that, the joy of our service will burst forth, and Jesus will feed the flock—those beautiful sheep for whom we are responsible—through us.

That's what the Twelve did on that hillside when they were responsible for feeding five thousand people: they came to Jesus. Did they come to him first? Well, no, not in that moment. They devised their plan first, and it was a miserably poor plan. We would do well to learn from their error. Undaunted, Jesus initiated *his* plan, taking what his apostles had and performing a miracle.

We typically focus on Jesus during the exposition of this miracle, as we should; however, throughout this book, we will also examine the actions and words of the Twelve. We will see how Jesus trained them and how they

---

[1]. Oswald Chambers, *My Utmost for His Highest, Updated Edition*, (Oswald Chambers Publications Association, Ltd, 1992). June 11

embraced that training to be godly servants. They served well that day and continued serving for the rest of their lives, as will we. Let's appropriate Jesus' training and follow the example of the Twelve. These twelve men were the leaders of the church in the first century, and I dare say, it was because they learned what being a servant means. As we put into practice what being a godly leader looks like, we will also master being humble servants.

Questions for Discussion

1. Where are you currently serving Jesus' sheep?

2. Would you describe your service as good or godly?

3. Do you see yourself as a leader? Why or why not?

4. What do you find most challenging about godly service?

5. Which of the ten traits of godly leaders would you say you possess or practice?

6. Which godly leadership trait would you like to develop more fully?

7. Describe a person you think is a godly servant leader. What about them do you most admire?

Chapter 2

Begin with Jesus

*Therefore, brothers, be all the more diligent
to confirm your calling and election, for if
you practice these qualities you will never fall.*
2 Peter 1:10

Have you looked up some slang words that middle-schoolers use today? Give it a try. Some make no sense, and I'm not even sure if some are words or merely sounds, let alone how to spell them! Then, use those words (as an adult) around the younger generation. They will laugh in your face. It is absurd. It is almost as absurd as when our parents tried to use our slang words. The older generation just doesn't get it. The same concept is at work within the church.

The world is changing at a dizzying speed; the pendulum of culture swings in ever-increasing arcs, and the church must keep up to stay relevant. Or should it? Servant leaders in the church must not fall behind. Behind what? Two thousand years ago, things changed dramatically, too, but nothing caught Jesus off guard then, and nothing catches him off guard today. Jesus was relevant then, and he is relevant now. When Jesus walked the earth, he orchestrated the changes necessary in leadership, and he continues to do so now. Today, like the Twelve, we must begin where we are and let Jesus change us into the leaders we need to become, instead of trying to appropriate whatever worldly thing we think we need to stay relevant. It all starts with Jesus.

What was it like to be in Jesus' inner circle as the world was being set on fire by the most fantastic Teacher ever? How must it have felt to witness

Jesus perform miracles, cast out demons, and speak with unabashed authority? To see the world turn on its heels? Let's go find out.

The disciples were riding high. They had returned from a successful mission campaign and were eager to report their success to Jesus and celebrate. Like most of us are when we've had a moment breathing the rarified air of a spiritual mountaintop, they didn't seem to be in a hurry to make the descent. They were ready to keep going, to march successfully from one assignment to the next, anxious to prove to Jesus that they were more than fit for whatever task he had in mind. Aren't we like that after experiencing a spiritual high? Who wants to stop and rest when there is much to do? If we slow down, we will get left behind. We will become obsolete. Irrelevant. But is that what is most important?

Perhaps we are a lot like the disciples. We want to move forward as quickly as possible with whatever new program or formula works before we get left behind. There are many hurting people in the world, and we want to reach them before we get too old, too out of touch, too irrelevant, or even obsolete.

Jesus sees things more clearly. He knew these men needed to overcome their desire for busyness, release their fight against falling behind, and refresh in him before they could continue to move ahead in his business. Jesus knew that if they persisted in leadership, ministry, or service without taking time with him to refresh, rest in his presence, and regroup, they would quickly give out or slowly burn out. The Twelve needed to embrace Jesus' presence.

Embracing Jesus' presence is also the first thing we need to be godly leaders.

In our zeal to work for Jesus, do we miss his call to hold up and relax? In our desperation to stay relevant, have we forgotten who holds the entire world in his hands? In our haste to change the world, do we forget who changed us? Do we let our spiritual reservoir dry up even as we try to flood the sphere of our influence with the fragrance of Jesus? If we are empty of Jesus, we have nothing spiritual to offer the culture or the church. There is so much in this world that depletes our spiritual reservoirs. To move forward effectively, we must regularly allow ourselves to be refilled. The only way to do that is to sit awhile with Jesus.

While we may overlook the connection between busyness and spiritual depletion, we seem to be in good company; the Twelve also missed it.

The apostles returned to Jesus and told him all that they had done and taught. And he said to them, "Come away by yourselves to a desolate place and rest a while." For many were coming and going, and they had no leisure even to eat. And they went away in the boat to a desolate place by themselves (Mark 6:30–32).

We all have both surface needs and profoundly deep needs. We easily recognize our surface needs: light, air, water, food, rest, shelter, clothing, and relationships. Jesus knows our deepest needs. He knows them better than we do because our souls have a depth we cannot reach by our own will or thoughts. This deepest part of our being is only accessible to God; in this depth, he works and speaks. We become aware of how he meets and ministers to us there as we see the results manifest in our thoughts and actions. Though we might not be consciously aware of God at work in the depths of our conscience, his presence is unmistakably revealed to us as his transforming work rises to take its place in the living out of our lives.

As we spend time with Jesus, God accomplishes his work of maturing and continually refining us. Our desire for more of God, closer intimacy with him, and a greater understanding of His Word and teaching originates in this deep place of our souls. The only way these longings and desires can be fulfilled is by spending time with Jesus. For that to happen, we need to recognize and defeat busyness. If we don't have time to begin with Jesus, we don't have time to begin.

If You Want to Do Great Things for Jesus,
You Must Spend Great Time with Jesus

The Twelve were soon to embark on the most significant work of their lives; they just weren't aware of it yet. As busy as they were going to be, they needed a solid grounding to begin. Jesus led them to set everything aside and spend time with him. To fully understand and embrace all of the training Jesus accomplished on that mountainside, we need to understand the busyness of the events leading up to the miracle. The Gospels tell us what was going on:

And he [Jesus] went about among the villages teaching. And he called the twelve and began to send them out two by two, and gave them authority over the unclean spirits... So they went out and proclaimed that people should repent. And they cast out many demons and anointed with oil many who were sick and healed them (Mark 6:6b-7, 12-13).

Not only had the Twelve obeyed by going, but they had experienced great success by driving out many (not just a few, but many!) demons and healing many people. Imagine the power, joy, and depth of love for others and for Jesus that they must have felt. They likely believed this power was the precursor to the roles they would undoubtedly hold when Jesus would soon reign as the ultimate King over this world, with each of them by his side. We know from Scripture that these men were fully human with fully human aspirations and had argued about who among them was the greatest and who would sit next to Jesus when Jesus sat upon his throne. Was the time near? Was this successful trip a sign that it was imminent? Indeed, it was a time to celebrate great, stunning triumphs.

The joy of the Twelve as they were recounting their victories was balanced by great heartache. Jesus was not sitting quietly waiting for these men to return. He was busy teaching and preaching in the villages of Galilee (Matthew 10:1, 11:1), and it was then that Jesus heard the news that Herod had murdered John the Baptist, his cousin and friend. John was the one who had identified Jesus to the world as the Lamb of God; he was the one who had baptized Jesus to fulfill all righteousness and who prepared the way for Jesus by preaching and calling for people to repent. This was a time of grave sorrow. So while Jesus was ready to celebrate with the Twelve, he was also in mourning.

Jesus, though fully God, was also fully human, and he experienced the complete impact of the crashing waves of grief that wash over us when a loved one dies. Perhaps Jesus even felt the loss more deeply because he more fully understood death. He grasped the fatigue of mourning that he and the Twelve would experience, and he knew the disciples needed time away. He understood that he did as well.

Jesus knows we become vulnerable to the enemy's attacks and schemes in our most emotional times, so he called for time to regroup, refresh, reconnect, and recount all that had happened. The Twelve needed time with Jesus to debrief and process the past before moving appropriately into the future. Stepping away to be with God was necessary for the Twelve to be able to place the events of their mission trip and John's death in proper perspective. Life can be challenging and confusing, and time away with Jesus is one of the keys to restoring or finding clarity. Before we can feed others, we must allow Jesus to feed us. Before we can adequately serve others, we must consent to being served by the One who came to serve. If we don't, our limited spiritual resources will not sustain us.

The Twelve did not come up with the idea to get away with Jesus; Jesus did. He was training them to recognize their need for rest and understand that only restoration in him can meet that need. We must refresh with Jesus both before and after we minister to others.

We probably all agree that spending time with Jesus before we serve is necessary. Most of us are accustomed to taking at least a few minutes for prayer, because we don't want to rush out without asking him to order and bless our service. But it is just as important to commune with him afterward, when we feel either the most filled up, fired up, and ready to move forward or the most depleted, burnt out, and prepared to quit. The fact is, if we forge ahead without regrouping and refreshing with Jesus, our zeal will eventually fizzle or flame out. When we pause and replenish, Jesus prepares us for what the next moments will require of us. We have no idea what tomorrow, or even the rest of today, will bring, but Jesus does.

The particulars of Jesus' conversation with the Twelve are not recorded. However, considering the grief surrounding John's death, coupled with the rejoicing of their authority over the demonic realm—the realm of destruction and death, I suspect Jesus used those moments to focus on life—eternal life. For eternal life is available only in Jesus.

Later in Luke, when the seventy-two disciples that Jesus had sent out to share what they had learned returned from their mission trip, they were rejoicing that the demons had submitted to them in Christ Jesus' name. But Jesus told them, *"Nevertheless, do not rejoice in this, that the spirits are subject to you, but rejoice that your names are written in heaven"* (Luke 10:20). It seems plausible that Jesus went over the same training at that moment: the reality of eternal life in him. His followers needed to understand that nothing on earth—no success, victory, or fame—is more important or more relevant than their status in heaven as recipients of eternal life, which comes only through Jesus. The Twelve needed a greater understanding of Jesus and a more complete awareness of their identity in Jesus. So do we.

Who is this Jesus who met with the Twelve? He is the same Jesus whom the Word of God tells us is *the Son of Man [who] came to seek and to save the lost* (Luke 19:10), who came *not to be served but to serve, and to give his life as a ransom for many* (Matthew 20:28).

This Son of Man, the One who came to serve—to seek and save the lost—is the One in whom we must place our trust. Once we believe in Jesus, we become God's children, and our name is written in the Book of Life, assuring us of a place in heaven with him for eternity. Only when we have received this status as God's children can we serve others effectively.

So, let's be clear: Before we can serve anyone in Christ's name, we must make our calling and election sure. In other words, we need to belong to him, ensuring our names are written in the Book of Life. There is only one way for that to happen: We must go away with him to the cross and conduct this private business of committing our entire lives and eternity to him. When we have accepted Jesus as our Savior and Lord, we will know beyond knowing that we are his. Do you have that assurance? Have you made your calling and election sure?

Heart Check

Asking if your election is sure may seem like a frivolous question in a book about godly leadership. But if we desire to serve others in the church, surely we must be Christians. Not everyone who assumes they are saved truly is. It is possible to deceive ourselves and others by making assumptions that are not grounded in facts. Christianity requires faith, and God gives us ample facts upon which to base our faith. Saving faith is not being *hopeful* that the things we read about Jesus are true; saving faith is putting our trust in our Savior—being *certain* that what he says is true—even when we don't fully understand it. So, I ask again: Are you saved? Do you know for certain? It's worth it to contemplate *how* you know.

We can only go further after this is settled—we must get this right, right from the start. Perhaps you can't recall a day when you did not know about Jesus, you've always gone to church, or your family has always practiced Christianity; so you are considering skipping the following few paragraphs because you feel confident you are saved. Despite this, I encourage you to read the following paragraphs carefully. If not for your benefit, then for the benefit of those you will serve.

Take some time and consider the following questions:

- When did you personally come to faith?

- When did you ask Jesus to save you from sin and be your Savior?

- Have you had a moment when you chose to stop leaning on your own strength and surrender your life to him, giving him unhindered reign over your life as you received him as your Lord, as God (John 1:12)?

Were you able to answer those questions? Inviting Jesus into your heart is a monumental decision that cannot be undone, and it is worth remembering. After all, it is a choice that changes everything! It transforms how you will live today and where you will spend eternity. Do you recall ever making this choice to give your life to Christ? If not, why not make it today? Even now, as you read this, why not choose *this* moment to make your calling and election sure? Tell Jesus that you are a sinner who cannot save yourself, and ask him to come into you through the Person of the Holy Spirit, to live in and through you, and to save you in himself for all eternity.

I recall being drawn to Jesus when I was a child. I was at a baptism service with my grandmother and sensed I was supposed to be baptized. No one had explained baptism or salvation to me. I knew the basics of heaven and hell, and I knew that I didn't want to go to hell when I died. In that moment, I felt called to align with those who were being baptized.

After the service, I told my grandmother, who then told my mom and dad. Soon, I was caught up in a whirlwind of baptismal preparations. I got a new dress and memorized the answers to some questions I'd be asked during the ceremony. I felt pretty confident after I was baptized that I was saved. I was told that I was. As I sat in the pew afterward, I recall thinking that I had to be as good as possible and always make every effort to attend church. In my 9-year-old mind, I committed to walking to church every Sunday morning if necessary (which I never did). In my 9-year-old mind, and with limited understanding, I believed I belonged to God.

Had I entered salvation through a performance plan? Was Jesus a harsh taskmaster who kept a record of my failings? Was he my get-out-of-hell-free card? I didn't know who Jesus was, but I assumed I was his and called myself a Christian. But nothing changed. Well, nothing except I was a bit more self-righteous and probably wielded that attribute proudly and more frequently than I should have.

My hiccup was that I didn't commit to surrender everything to Jesus (everything: my desires, my will, my hopes, my dreams, my life). No one told me about that part. I just knew I had grown up in a family that regularly attended church, which seemed to be the key to salvation. I assumed I was saved because I knew the Sunday school songs and Bible stories and was now baptized. Yet, Jesus was not my Lord. He was not the King in whose army I fought. He was simply Jesus: the baby in the manger at Christmas, the man on the cross on Good Friday, and the One missing from the tomb on Easter Sunday morning. He was the Cosmic-Go-To in times of trouble when I needed help. He was the One to bargain with in desperation. He was not the One who led me into green pastures or protected me from ravenous wolves. He also made me feel miserable when I didn't do what I knew I should. Sin? I never really thought much about sin, at least not my own. I wasn't that bad, but I often asked for forgiveness when I prayed before bed. I was a good student. I respected my parents (most of the time). And later, I went to a Christian college where I met a Christian man, got married, and had precious babies. I taught in Sunday school and Vacation Bible School. I was not nearly as bad as some people I knew; those people were sinners! And, besides, any sin I had committed was forgiven; I was pretty sure about that because the Bible told me that my sin was removed from me *as far as the east is from the west* (Psalm 103:12).

Was I saved? Some would say I was not because I had not submitted to Jesus as Lord. I believe I was because of the precious doctrine of election. God had a hold on me and would not let me go. In my child-like understanding, I loved Jesus, and I was his. The proof was that the Holy Spirit didn't let me get away with sin without intense conviction. I must confess, though, that I didn't understand the difference between conviction and condemnation. Rather than repent (which conviction leads to), I absolved myself of guilt by reminding myself that *there is…no condemnation for those who are in Christ Jesus* (Romans 8:1), and I proceeded to live however I thought best benefited me.

Was I in Christ Jesus? I had no power or freedom. I could not change myself. Instead, I just kept trying to do what I thought others expected of me—plugging along in my various service and leadership roles. As I did, I experienced temporary happiness, but never enduring joy. Additionally, my initial enthusiasm always seemed to wane quickly. Was Jesus both my Savior and my Lord? No. I wanted him as my Savior; I wasn't ready to let him be my Lord.

It pleased me to keep Jesus in the doorway where I could hear his knocking, but I didn't want to let him in. It was easier if I just kept him close to the door; that way, I could go out and chat with him when I needed counsel or high-five him when I did something super-religious. I was able to sit next to him when I was hurting and plead with him when I needed help. But if I surrendered to him, I knew he would want to come into every room, and there were rooms where I didn't want him. I knew that if I genuinely submitted my life to him, he would come in as Lord of the manor, and where would that leave me?

Did I have a relationship with him? Yes. Was it a saving relationship? Before I answer that, let me pause and reiterate that I'm retelling the salvation story of a 9-year-old, but I am not writing to 9-year-olds. I am writing to adults who desire to be godly servants. Perhaps you were saved as a child, as I thought I was, and nothing changed for you, either. If, however, as an adult, you have not experienced the conviction of the Holy Spirit throughout your life or felt the presence of God guiding and directing you, if you have not grown and matured in your faith and are still living your life as *you* see fit, rebelling against the Lordship of Jesus, then perhaps you are not saved. Jesus doesn't save us to put us in his trophy case. He saves us so he can have a relationship with us and use us for his glory. As you mature, you must submit to God as Lord and love him and honor him as your Savior. He will not let us get away with treating him as only our get-out-of-hell-free card forever.

We must honor Jesus as *both* our Lord and our Savior, or he is neither. I think that is what he means when he says, *"Not everyone who says to me, 'Lord, Lord' will enter the kingdom of heaven, but the one who does the will of my Father who is in heaven"* (Matthew 7:21). I had much to learn and understand about who Jesus was before I could surrender all to him. Still, God had a hold of me as a child, and he would not let go. I also now know that making a profession of faith and being baptized is not the end but the beginning. Jesus will pursue us, longing for our surrender, but he will not pursue us forever. Have you surrendered to him?

The day Jesus became my Lord, I finally understood that it was Jesus who saved me from my sinful self. Just like you, I was born a sinner, so sinning was what I did. I could never change my heart; only God could, and only as I asked him. So, I asked Jesus to save me and invited him in, in the Person of the Holy Spirit, to heal and restore me to wholeness and to regenerate my dead spirit into new life (Ephesians 2:1-10). I appealed to his Word: *But God, being rich in mercy, because of the great love with which he loved us, even when we were dead in our trespasses, made us alive together with Christ—by grace you have been saved* (Ephesians 2:4-5). And, at that moment—some would say that was the moment of my salvation—in gratitude for saving me (whether twenty years earlier as a 9-year-old or on that day as a 29-year-old), I surrendered and submitted to him as my Lord.

When Jesus saves us, he unites us with himself and promises to live within us throughout our lives. But there must be a death of self for there to be new life in Christ. By dying to self, then, and only then, does Jesus reign as Lord. What is a lord? The boss. The boss of me. The one who, when he says, "Jump," we ask, "How high?" after our feet have left the ground. It must be as Jesus said: *"If anyone would come after me, let him deny himself and take up his cross daily and follow me. For whoever would save his life will lose it, but whoever loses his life for my sake will save it"* (Luke 9:23-24).

Jesus must be Lord and Savior, both or neither. Is he yours? Do you recall when your life changed, when you were born again? This birth is *not of blood nor of the will of the flesh nor of the will of man, but of God* (John 1:13). It is accomplished through the regenerating power of the Holy

Spirit. You cannot will yourself into a regenerated person; only God has the power to cause you to be born again.

Do you remember when your name was recorded in the Book of Life? It is a day far more important than your physical birthday; it is infinitely more important than your wedding anniversary and eternally more important than any other day of your life. If you don't know the day or the season of life you were in when you decided to receive Jesus as your Savior and your Lord, there is grave danger that you are assuming that you have fully submitted to Christ when you have not.

Not only should you be able to recall the time or season when you decided to receive Jesus, but your life should reflect the commitment. Does it? Is there anything about your life that proves you are a Christian? Is there fruit, a harvest of righteousness, a change from who you were to who you are, such that people see you and know you belong to Jesus? Do you reflect Jesus' ways, values, love, and life? Making a decision is only the beginning; committing to that decision is proof that the decision is real.

Have you come away with Jesus? Have you met him at the cross? Or are you living as a Christian simply because it is all you've ever known, because someone else prayed for you, or because, like me, there was a time when it seemed right to be baptized or confirmed? If you are not sure of your salvation, there is a danger that you could be eternally lost.

Before we can serve others, Christ Jesus, our Lord, must serve us. He served us on the cross, paying our sin debt, but we must appropriate it for ourselves. We must accept his gift of life. Otherwise, we will starve to death trying to feed his sheep. If we've not surrendered to Jesus and there is no eternal life in us, then we have nothing to give except the finite mortal lives we live, and we will quickly run out of that.

Is he asking you today, "Come away with me?" Will you, on this day, make your calling and election sure? If you are not born again, regenerated to a new life, then the rest of this book will only add to your frustration. We have no power to follow Jesus, do what he calls us to, or be the people we were created to be unless we have the power of Jesus within us through the indwelling Holy Spirit. Jesus must be both our Savior and our Lord.

Reality Check

As saved sinners, our hearts overflow with love for our Lord, and we desire to serve him. But we will only be successful as we work in the power of Christ. His words make it clear, *"I am the vine; you are the branches. Whoever abides in me and I in him, he it is that bears much fruit, for apart from me you can do nothing"* (John 15:5). We cannot bear spiritual fruit or serve his kingdom effectively apart from him. Oh, sure, we can do some things and do them quite well. Some of us are adept at doing many things well. Nevertheless, the accomplishments and accolades of a life—even a life of service—lived apart from Christ will have no eternal value. It will count for nothing. Therefore, like the Twelve, we must continually abide in Christ Jesus.

The Twelve had just returned from a mission trip where they had encountered evil, cast out demons, and healed many people. Those successes don't happen in a spiritual vacuum; therefore, the Twelve must have been targets of the opposition, of the evil one. If we are going to be servants of Jesus, going to be about the business of feeding his sheep, then we can expect that we will show up on the radar screen of Satan. He will understand our motivation and intent, and he will do all he can to make us ineffective. We may not be big enough targets to attract Satan himself, but we will surely attract the attention of his minions.

The goal of the evil one is to keep us from serving God's people; he wrote the book on that and has an almost limitless supply of weapons. But we must never forget that, though he is powerful, Satan is already defeated.

Jesus defeated him at the cross, and his time is limited. Perhaps that's why he works so hard. Still, he is a worthy opponent who has many tools to try to defeat, derail, discourage, destroy, deceive, and distract us.

The evil one will try to make us feel defeated in an attempt to subdue us. We are in danger of giving in when we forget the power we hold in Christ against internal turmoil such as fear, weakness, self-doubt, and shame. Satan also expertly uses external attacks—such as legal issues, finances, or even weather—to wage war against us. He thinks that if the hurdles are too high, we won't try to jump them. We must remember, however, that as children of the omnipotent, omnipresent, all-powerful God, we are *more than conquerors* (Romans 8:37) through Christ Jesus.

The forces of evil will attempt to derail us and get us off track. Satan is good at that, and we live in his realm, the world, and are susceptible to his wiles. Though we may, in our humanity, be prone to panic and knee-jerk reactions, we can stand firm as we focus on Jesus. Jesus' Word must be the rail upon which our train glides. As we trust in him, he will keep our paths straight and light our way.

Satan will attempt to destroy us, but we have already died with Christ. Therefore, any other destruction is temporary. Satan may attack our reputation or programs, but those are nothing when our identity is in Christ rather than ourselves or our programs. We are potent as we abide in Christ Jesus our Lord.

Discouragement is a powerful tool of the evil one, which Oswald Chambers defines as "disillusioned self-love." Self-love is the kind of love the world tells us we must have before we can love anyone else. What a great victory the evil one procures when he lures us into spending more time and energy telling *ourselves* we are worthy than using that time to tell God that *he* is worthy. But we can defeat Satan and overcome discouragement by focusing on our God and spending less time thinking of ourselves. The self, that little god we battle daily, is defeated only as the God of the universe rules in our hearts; this is key to defeating discouragement.

Satan, the father of lies, will attempt to deceive us. He is a roaring lion—boastful, loud, and on the prowl, looking for someone to devour with his deception. Therefore, we must study God's Word to know and embrace the truth so that the deceptive traps of evil do not ensnare us.

Satan will try to distract us. While we may not guard against this ploy, be assured it is one of his most effective weapons. If he can't cause us to sin, destroy us, deceive us, or derail us, he'll keep us busy. One of his trickiest moves is to use the Lord's business, the Lord's people, and what we consider our service to the Lord as distractions to keep us from hearing directly from God and doing his true will.

When we are too busy to come away with Christ before we serve him, we surrender to the enemy before we even start. Nevertheless, we are not alone in our endeavors to resist him. It is not easy, and we will sometimes fall victim to his advances, but we don't have to hand him the victory; we have the power to resist him within us. James, the brother of Jesus, tells us to *resist the devil, and he will flee from you,* and he states the primary means of resisting him is to *draw near to God* (James 4:7-8). We do not have to succumb to Satan's devices. Being aware of the tactics he uses helps us stand against him.

Satan is real, and he uses the ordinary things in our lives to accomplish his plans and attempt to thwart God's plans. When Joseph was thrown into the pit and sold to slave traders, his brothers were carrying out a wicked intention to harm him. Yet somehow, in the very same act, God had good intentions—the saving of many lives (Genesis 50:20). We experience this same duality of intentions—the intent of the evil one for wickedness and of God for good—as we seek to serve those God places in our paths. If the evil one can separate us from Jesus, our service is doomed. We overcome busyness by taking time alone with Jesus and surrendering to him and his direction. Surrendering to Jesus arms us for victory.

While we must be aware of our enemy, we can be encouraged and assured of our victory when we are united in Christ as believers. Christ Jesus has all authority over evil. Satan is not omniscient, omnipotent, or omnipresent; only God is. Satan may attempt to defeat us, but he is a defeated foe; he has no power over us that God does not allow. Satan's power, therefore, is limited and held within the confines of God's sovereignty. Cosmic wars are raging, but every battle is fought in God's hands, and the war has already been won. We do not have to fear; we died and now are *hidden with Christ in God* (Colossians 3:3). If we are hidden with (surrendered to) Christ, nothing can harm us.

Because of the work that our Lord Jesus Christ accomplished on our behalf on the cross, we can *with confidence draw near to the throne of grace, that we may receive mercy and find grace to help in time of need* (Hebrews 4:16). We are never on our own; we are never alone. We always have access to the spiritual weapons we need to fight *against the rulers, against the authorities, against the cosmic powers over this present darkness, against the spiritual forces of evil in the heavenly places* (Ephesians 6:12). We are never without access to God, who is our shield and has every resource in the universe at his disposal. Successful service is probable as we stay connected to Jesus, the True Vine.

If we want to be fed well and be able to feed others, we must draw up the nourishment we need from the Vine. It is from the Vine that we derive our nutrition. Like a hungry child who knows where the food is but is too small to reach the cupboard, we must use every means available to us to access the nutrition in Jesus. It is not enough to know him; we must spend time with him in prayer, and we must study his Word. We need to get involved in Bible studies that use the Bible as the primary resource. We must connect with a church where the pastor teaches from God's Word weekly. We need spiritual mentors and friends who help us learn to study and hold us accountable for spending time with Jesus. His nutrients are infinite. He will never run out, nor will we, as long as we stay connected to him. If we are not connected to Jesus, all other motivation, energy, strength, wisdom, and spiritual food sources will quickly be depleted. Only in Christ Jesus has God given us all we need for success, including relevance.

Jesus knows us better than we know ourselves. He knew the Twelve. He recognized it was essential for them to get away on a beautiful spring day to spend some time with him before the next thing, which only he saw coming. The Twelve needed to separate themselves from the world and spend time with God. Only he could provide the necessary refreshment and the assurance that they belonged to him. Before they moved forward, it was vital for the Twelve to experience the all-consuming presence of God.

If we do not take time to get away with Jesus but rather forge ahead in our fast-fading energy, our endeavors cannot succeed as God intends. Even when we feel they do succeed, we must ask by whose standard we are measuring success: the world's or God's? If God is not with us, our accomplishments will look no different than any other secular endeavor or program. How will anyone know that we belong to God if they do not see God with us, in us, and through us as we serve his people? The King we surrender to is the one whom we serve. Apart from him, our service is merely a distraction that keeps us busy.

The Twelve did not know what was right around the corner; Jesus did. And he was preparing them for it. We do not know what tomorrow holds, but Jesus does. The most reasonable thing we can do is spend time with Jesus, allowing him to train us and align our priorities with his before we march into the future. Jesus' presence will rise to its proper place in our lives and reveal itself to others as we spend time with him. Don't be afraid to seek his presence and wait for his direction.

Jesus was accessible to the Twelve; he was always in their midst; apart from him, they could do nothing. Yet the Twelve went up a hill to talk and refresh with Jesus, and before the end of the day, they will have become sacred go-betweens. Something extraordinary was about to happen in the lives of the Twelve and the lives of well over five thousand additional souls on a beautiful spring day in Israel. The Twelve were about to experience a challenge that would overwhelm them. Their lives and perspectives would never be the same. Their understanding of Jesus would grow exponentially. All because they first took time to get away with Jesus, going where he led them, listening to what he had to say, and preparing for those who would soon arrive.

Jesus is accessible to us, too; he is in our midst and inside of us. Like the Twelve, we can do nothing of any eternal value apart from him. And we also have no idea what is in store for us tomorrow; none of us does. Isn't it best to get away with Jesus so that we are prepared for whatever wonderfully spectacular thing he already knows is right around the corner? If we want to do great things with Jesus or for Jesus, we must spend great time with him because we love him and desire to serve his people. Are you preparing to become a sacred go-between?

To become godly leaders who feed Jesus' sheep with assurance, **we must first begin with Jesus**. *We must repent of attempting to serve others in our own way and for our purposes. As we trust God to serve us before we serve others, we will overcome the frustrations of the evil one and the busyness of life. Then we will be prepared to accomplish all that God has for us.*

Questions for Discussion

1. Is Jesus both your Savior and your Lord? Upon what are you basing your assurance?

2. Do you have a place to meet with Jesus? Do you have an unbreakable appointment?

3. How well do you know your enemy? Can you recognize his tactics, twists, and turns as he attempts to defeat you? To which of his attacks are you most vulnerable?

4. Do you "suit up" before you go out for battle? Do you know how to put on the armor of God to withstand the evil that will come against you?

5. What tools are you utilizing to acquire as many nutrients as possible from the True Vine?

6. Are you prepared for earth-shattering change? For the spectacular? For the out-of-the-ordinary? Will you get away with Jesus to prepare for whatever he has for you?

7. How is Jesus aligning your priorities and perspective with his?

Chapter 3

Hone Your Vision

We look not to the things that are seen but to the things that are unseen. For the things that are seen are transient, but the things that are unseen are eternal.
2 Corinthians 4:18

No one attends a concert to hear the backup singers (except maybe the backup singers' moms), and no one in the crowd who followed Jesus came to see the disciples. I wonder if the Twelve, who were enjoying the solitude, the mutual comfort in their grief, and the undivided attention of Jesus, saw the crowd as a nuisance. Did they like what they saw? What, exactly, did they see? Intruders? Distractions? People who wanted Jesus or what Jesus could do for them? Crowds who desired the spectacular over the spiritual? The Scriptures tell us that the people who showed up that day came because they saw the way he healed the sick (John 6:2). Yet, was there something deep within the people's souls, perhaps deeper than they were aware, that was hungry for God? Was their need beyond their understanding and outside the vision of the Twelve?

This was an intense time for Jesus' apostles. They had experienced spiritual success on the road and desired to debrief with Jesus. They also had to process the death of John. There was much to discuss, but there was no time or place for discussion. So many people were coming and going that the Twelve didn't even have time to eat, let alone refresh with Jesus. So Jesus took them away to a quiet place where they could be taught—or so they thought. However, Jesus led them to a place where he would offer them a lesson in seeing as he sees, as he clarified their marred perception.

Now many saw them going and recognized them, and they ran there on foot from all the towns and got there ahead of them. When he [Jesus] went ashore he saw a great crowd, and he had compassion on them, because they were like sheep without a shepherd. And he began to teach them many things (Mark 6:33-34).

In direct opposition to their expectations, Jesus took the Twelve to what turned out to be a crowded hillside rather than a solitary place. Jesus would be with the Twelve, but they would have to share him as he ministered to the crowd. Additionally, the apostles had yet to eat—I'm sure they probably were not as gracious and hospitable as they could have been, but I'll extend grace because I feel confident I would have been frustrated, too.

There Is Always More to See Than We Can See

It is challenging to look beyond the physical to perceive people's deeper needs, especially when we have our own needs. However, as servants in the church, we must consider what we cannot see. We must learn to hone our vision so we can appreciate people as Jesus does. We must let him teach us, just as he taught the Twelve.

The Twelve saw people trying to get a glimpse of the most celebrated preacher of their day: They wanted to see the One who could heal their sick, the One who was noted for his miraculous performances, the One many of them had reduced to a showman. It wasn't just the Twelve who had imperfect vision. There is a lesson for us here: What we see with our human, physical eye is only a portion of what there is to see. And the lens through which we view the ordinary or the spectacular determines how we respond to it.

Just as many in the multitude could not see who Jesus, the Son of God, was, neither can we. And, like them, because we don't see clearly, we reduce God to what is manageable or what we want him to be. To become godly servants, we must continually guard against reducing God to celebrity status or academic pursuit. God is not a thrilling show or a spectacle. He is the Almighty who created us with a desire to know all there is to know about him. Our hearts cry out to know him. Like the crowds, we seek him, even without having full awareness of all he is or whom we seek.

Nevertheless, when we cannot fully comprehend what our spirit desires, we attempt to satiate our hunger that yearns, craves, and cries out for God by feeding ourselves little morsels of religion, spirituality, or philosophy. And often, we settle for what we can see and understand with our finite minds and diminished vision. Then, because our image of God is limited, our perception of God's people, those he is bringing to us to serve, is also limited. Since *he has put eternity into man's heart,* we, like the crowd that day, long to know the eternal, yet we *cannot find out what God has done from the beginning to the end* (Ecclesiastes 3:11). God is so much more than we can embrace, yet, he welcomes our presence, and encourages us by revealing himself in ways we can understand. Therefore, we must continually allow our vision of God to expand as we study who he is in His Word and experience him in our lives. If we don't actively seek to understand who God is and who Jesus is, we will remain shortsighted, like the Twelve were when they looked out upon the crowd. We must learn to see as Jesus sees.

What did Jesus see on that hillside? Where the Twelve saw a distraction, Jesus saw sheep without a shepherd. The Twelve saw their quiet afternoon being wiped away, but Jesus recognized the opportunity to wipe away misery and pain. The Twelve saw a miracle-seeking crowd, and Jesus got excited at having a chance to plant seeds of faith through the miraculous. While the Twelve saw a nuisance, Jesus was fully aware of hurting, lost, and straying souls. The Twelve saw throngs of undeserving people; Jesus knew He had an opportunity to dispense grace—God's favor on the undeserving. Jesus also saw the motives of the crowd. He was not naïve; he knew these people were thrill-seekers who had not come because they were pursuing his presence, but because they were intrigued with what he might do or give to them. He recognized that, for the most part, the individuals in the crowd were consumers, out to get what they could. Yet, Jesus saw through the hardened shells of the lost souls before him, had compassion for them, and met their needs.

Like Jesus, we must see beyond others' immaturity and false understandings, and choose to serve their needs. Despite the crowd being undeserving and misguided, the disciples should have been excited that they had the opportunity to point so many to Jesus, the true thrill-giver. And that should be our attitude, as well. After all, Jesus always has been and always will be the main attraction; we are blessed to be his backup singers.

Like the Twelve on the hillside with Jesus, we long to get away with Jesus. We think we deserve time alone with him, so we sit down in our quiet place with our Bibles open, ready to drink in God's Word deeply. Then come the interruptions: a notification ping, a phone rings, a child runs in, or a spouse needs to talk. It is not unlike the evil one to use people we love to distract us. But it is also not unlike God to use people we love to prompt us to put the things we are learning into practice. If we have done all that we can to provide uninterrupted time with the Lord (phones silenced, door closed, computer off) and are then interrupted, we can trust that God will use the distraction to train us, even while Satan is working to distract us. The evil one gains victory when we allow the distraction to distract us from God. However, when the distraction draws us closer to God, as this situation will with the Twelve, we know that God is utilizing the distraction for his glory and training us for our good. He is clarifying our vision.

This event is a time of training for the Twelve; every situation and every interaction is an opportunity for training. Either we are being trained, or we are training others. How we respond in any given moment reveals what we have learned and what we have yet to learn. Do we respond with grace, like Jesus? Or do we bulldoze forward, seeking our own agenda, like so many in the crowd? Everything we do sets an example for others, of either honoring God or dishonoring him, believing and trusting him, or worrying and floundering in lack of belief and trust. In every encounter, we train people to draw close to God or move away from him. Jesus always leads us closer to God; now, he will teach the Twelve to do the same. By learning how to view people as Jesus does, we will learn how to lead them to God.

What We See Usually Determines Our Service

We must learn to see as Jesus sees if we are to serve his people in his way. We must see every difficult circumstance as an opportunity to point people to Jesus. However, most of us are like infants; our vision is limited—we see what is closest to us and find it nearly impossible to focus on anything in the distance. As flawed humans, we may understand the immediate problem and, perhaps, a one-sided solution, but we are often blind to the multifaceted consequences of that solution. We don't have the bird's eye view that God has. In our own wisdom, we can only survey things through the paradigm of our up-close circumstances and process the landscape through our biases and the limitations of our bent. The Twelve were hungry and wanted to be alone with Jesus. How would you react? How would I?

Our worldview determines how we react, and there are only two worldviews: One based on God's Word and the other based on man's words. Worldview is the way we perceive and understand reality. A God-based worldview allows us to see that God is at work in all things for our good and his eternal glory. A worldview based on man's words causes us to see things as random, arbitrary, or fated—with no definable good or bad. Our worldview influences not only how we perceive reality, but it also impacts how we react to what we see.

We often react with judgment when we look at life's events through the prism of our limited wisdom or a worldview not based on Scripture. Is that what the Twelve did? Did they assume the crowds were not believers and were not committed to following Christ? Did they make a judgment that the people were coming only to see what they could get, to be healed and witness the spectacular? Did they assume the people would take as much as Jesus would give them and probably not even stay around long enough to say "Thank you"?

Is this how we judge the hurting people whom God places before us? It makes sense that we would. In American culture, we have been trained to hide our hurts, shame, and needs. Everyone wants to appear independent, strong, and successful; so we erect walls, making it difficult for anyone to see what we are hiding. On the other extreme, we may become accustomed to overcompensating by claiming victim status as we consider everything an offense, thus causing others to become immune to our problems while we hide our actual needs. Because of these false facades, combined with our worldview biases, is it any wonder we judge and serve errantly? However, when we refuse to clean our lenses by asking Jesus to allow us to see others as he sees them, our vision will continue to be blurry, and we will be unable to help others appropriately—that is, as Jesus calls us to. In our humanity, without the assistance of the Holy Spirit, we cannot see what others don't reveal, so we judge. And our judgment is often erroneously based on what we assume is hidden.

Because we don't fully understand what someone else is going through, we sometimes react with impatience. This was not a good time for the Twelve, but the crowds didn't know that; they were unaware of why Jesus and the Twelve had retreated to this quiet place. Jesus' need to escape with the Twelve was not on their radar. Still, the crowd didn't stop to ponder the idea that they were the intruders.

In impatience, we let our ire up because we quickly conclude that those who distract us are selfish, even though they probably have no idea they've imposed on us. When our impatience and intolerance taint our vision of others, we become unable to see their suffering and may fail to show kindness and forbearance. Focusing only on ourselves, how can we possibly love others as Jesus loves?

Sometimes, we react to distractions with frustration. We see a time-consuming crowd of selfish energy vampires drawing the lifeblood from us. We experience an emotional burden or feel pushed beyond our comfort zone, and our first thought is to erect safe boundaries because there are too many people with too many needs, and we don't have enough time, resources, or staff to take care of them. We may even internally respond: This is too much; can't they go away? But how can we see clearly when we allow frustration to cloud our vision?

We all may encounter circumstances when we react with aloofness, thinking, This is someone else's job; I can't do anything. We become blind to anyone's needs other than our own and to any pain that is not ours. So we turn away and assume someone else will step up, because someone always does.

Perhaps the crowd was blind to who Jesus was because they were only looking at his works. They wanted physical healing and, therefore, failed to recognize that the more critical healing they needed was much more profound.

Nevertheless, this was who God brought to Jesus and the Twelve. These were the people who needed to be served. God brings these same kinds of people to you and me.

But Jesus didn't just see the crowd. He saw *individuals* who happened to be in a crowd. He saw each of them clearly: They were his lost and hungry souls. His lost and hungry sheep. What is miraculous is that Jesus saw them the same way he saw you and me when we were sinners. We must remember that it was *while we were still weak, at the right time, Christ died for the ungodly.* You and me. *While we were still sinners, Christ died for us* (Romans 5:6, 8). Jesus did not see pagans; he did not see unbelievers who should get what they deserve; Jesus saw hopeless and helpless men, women, and children made in his image—the image of God—upon whom he would pour out his grace and for whom he soon would shed his blood. We must assume that every unbeliever God places before us may be a pre-Christian, someone we have the privilege of introducing to the Lord Jesus Christ.

The people coming to Jesus on this particular day came for physical rescue; they did not understand their need for spiritual rescue. They knew their wants but not their needs. They were undeserving of Jesus' love and compassion, yet that is precisely what they received.

Jesus looked out on the crowd with compassion: a deep guttural sense of sharing in their suffering. Jesus was moved by compassion. He saw reality: these were lost, struggling sheep with no one to protect or nurture them, no one to apply healing balm to their wounds or even feed them. They had been torn by hungry wolves and worldly predators who had taken all they had and left them defenseless. They were sheep lacerated by life's trials, left shredded, bleeding, and helpless; sheep without a safe pen to retreat to, a safety net of love and forgiveness to fall into, or a wall of defense to protect them from whatever the future held. Jesus saw the truth, and it moved him to the core.

We may sympathize with this crowd; we may even relate them to the individuals God brings to us. But we can still fall short of compassion—that deep, to the core sharing in their suffering. To have compassion, we must empathize, remembering that we each were lost, broken, battered sheep; at one time, you and I were someone else's distraction or interruption. We were as lost as the people in this crowd, as lost as the people God brings before us. We must carry this vision, remembering our pre-saved souls in this same state of lostness, to overcome our lack of compassion for others.

Jesus was not bound to meet anyone's needs: not the crowd's, not the disciples', not yours, and not mine. Yet he did. That is God's grace. Jesus extended grace to you and me when we were helpless and hopeless because he knew our needs and our inability to meet them. He knew we could not help ourselves because we could not earn God's favor. He saw that we were lost sheep; and he alone was—and is—the True Shepherd who can save us.

Jesus sees clearly. Jesus sees you and me accurately. He knows our motives, which, like the crowd's, are often wrong. Still, he meets our needs. Jesus compassionately and graciously poured love into each person in that crowd, just as he fed their bodies with food. As the Twelve participated, they began to understand and relate to each person with holy compassion; they saw the crowds as Jesus saw them, as individual lost souls. As we participate in Jesus' work, miraculously, our vision changes and begins to align with his.

Yet, no matter how well we see, we cannot see the contents of another's heart. Therefore, we are not to judge the hearts of those God brings to us. We are tasked with serving them and showing them the way to Jesus. To serve others, we must ask the Holy Spirit to allow us to see as Jesus sees and then seek to understand the need, rather than the circumstances.

If our focus is only on the circumstances we can see, without understanding the need, we will be tempted to effect change in the circumstances. We cannot know how God is working or how he might use us to meet the need—we must trust him and point the hurting soul to Jesus.

Even if we can change the circumstances, how do we know if our changes will improve the situation? For today? For tomorrow? Our role is to do as the Holy Spirit instructs us, trusting his provision.

As we trust the Holy Spirit and obey his leading, we can trust God to meet every need. God alone has the sufficient resources and wisdom to lift people out of pain, loss, difficulty, and need. His way is perfect. So even when we don't understand, we can have faith that he is doing a mighty work through suffering, lostness, hardship, and hopelessness. And rejoice that he often gives us the privilege of partnering with him to reach those in need.

Seeing Clearly Means Seeing That Jesus Meets Every Need

Like the Twelve, our natural inclination is to meet the needs we perceive through our physical eyes, but our vision is often clouded and limited by what we can physically see. Therefore, we probably won't understand the depth of the need in the people God brings to us to lead and serve. When our work flows out of the paradigm through which we view the world, how we serve is limited by what we think best meets the perceived need; that "best" often includes the effect on our own needs, wants, and desires. So we must learn to see beyond *our* circumstances and situations, so we can clearly see the needs of those we are called to serve. When we do, we will recognize that the greatest need for each person we serve is the recognition of and submission to Jesus.

Although we see the traps of muck and mire that bog people down, our goal must not simply be to rescue people from their difficulties and sufferings. We must point them to Jesus amid their problems and sorrows. As we share Jesus, we help them bear the weight of their trials and sufferings. We are not now, nor can we ever be, anyone's savior. We are merely the tools the Savior uses in whatever capacity he knows is best. He may use us to help change someone's circumstances or to help them endure their circumstances. Our primary responsibility is to show by example how to bring Jesus into a struggle. When we ask the Holy Spirit for guidance, we will know when and how to pray with and for others and what additional support we are to offer. Then, we can demonstrate our faith as we trust Jesus to lift them out or provide whatever they need to persevere. We must always see Jesus as sufficient to meet all our needs.

But what if we need convincing that Jesus is sufficient to meet the needs of suffering people? We say he is, but do we believe it? Why wouldn't we? Is it because we fail to see Jesus meeting our needs? We must see Jesus clearly in our own suffering before we can bring him into another's. We must understand how he ministers to us in our difficulties and hardships before we can convince anyone else that he is the One who can and will minister to them.

We see Jesus more clearly as we spend time with him in his Word, pray, come away with him, and turn to him in every part of our lives. Only then can we be sure that he is sufficient to meet our needs and the needs of others in every aspect of life. In our quiet time with Jesus, he trains us, speaks to us, and helps us see that he is what we need. As we spend time with Jesus, we are changed. As we spend time in his Word, as we choose to *not be conformed to this world, but be transformed by the renewal of [our] mind, [then] by testing, [we] may discern what is the will of God, what is good and acceptable and perfect* (Romans 12:1-2). This renewal of our minds, as we study God's Word and spend time with Jesus, transforms our worldview, moving us from merely seeing life's events as random to recognizing that God is at work in all things, making people who they are becoming, who he has called them to be.

When we rightly see ourselves as undeserving of God's grace—people with a limitless capacity for evil and wickedness, hopeless and helpless, unable to please God—only then can we begin to understand grace. As we recognize who we were in our helplessness and sin and that God chose to love and save us, we see how amazing grace truly is. Moreover, as we understand the grace we have received, we see more clearly our responsibility to extend grace to all others.

Seeing Ourselves as Workmen

God loved us when we were the most unlovely and unlovable. He loved us when we were at war with him. He loved us when we were sinners, and now he loves us as his children because he saved and adopted us as his own. And, amazingly, God has work for us to do. Not work that is a task to secure our salvation, but work that reflects our love for him and proves our salvation. *For we are his workmanship, created in Christ Jesus for good works, which God prepared beforehand, that we should walk in them* (Ephesians 2:10).

Our work may not arrive at a convenient time or in the way we would expect, and it could come as a distraction, just as it came to the Twelve, but God knows the best way to reveal the work he has called us to do. We are God's workmanship; he created us for and calls us into his service. That call usually comes through another person and will most likely be to a position he has already equipped us for. However, when the call is not spectacular or merely shows up like a crowd on a hillside on a spring day, how do we recognize it?

In Exodus 2, we read about Moses' poor vision. When Moses saw the Israelites struggling under their oppressors, he understood his calling was to rescue them. However, because of his limited vision, Moses did not see that the Israelites' actual need was to know God, so he instinctively acted on what he saw, killing an Egyptian. Moses didn't take time to allow God to hone his vision. If he had, he would have understood that his time of service had not yet arrived, and his calling was never to kill the Egyptian. Moses saw the immediate physical need, but couldn't envision that there was still much God needed to do—both in him and in the Israelites. Moses needed to learn to see God in the bigger picture.

Another man whose vision required honing was Peter. On the beach after Jesus' death and resurrection, Peter was more than ready for reinstatement, vowing three times to feed Jesus' sheep. Three times. Yet, we see in the Gospel of John that when Jesus told Peter his service would end in his own death and, despite this, commanded him to *"Follow me,"* Peter immediately turned around, looked at John, and then asked Jesus, *"What about this man?"* (John 21:15-21). Peter needed to have his focus fixed, to take his eyes off others and look only to Jesus.

Our work is not to be the focus; neither are we nor even the people we serve the focus. Jesus is always the focus, yet many of us need a focus fix. Jesus himself draws those who come to us, and we must strive to see them through his eyes. Our service is never about how great we are at meeting someone else's needs; it is about how good we are at showing others how great Jesus is. When Jesus corrects our vision, we will be able to see all people as he sees them: lost sheep who need a shepherd. As we accept his vision and push our own aside, we will no longer register racial, economic, cultural, or gender differences; we will appreciate that all people are created in God's image. We will observe people who are hurting, lost, and adrift, and understand that they need Jesus; nothing apart from him will satisfy them. When we attempt to meet the needs of others without offering them Jesus, we are merely providing a temporary Band-Aid. Making the hurting people we encounter aware of Jesus' presence must be our goal. That doesn't mean we preach a sermon before we offer food, love, comfort, or clothes; it means that everything we do is because we love Jesus and, therefore, we show love to his children.

We must serve each person God brings to us and be prepared to lead them to Jesus. The fields are ripe for the harvest, but if the worries of the day or our personal biases cloud our sight, we will not be able to see the field, let alone the ripe wheat. When Jesus told the disciples to pray for harvesters, they prayed. And who did Jesus send? He sent the disciples, the very people who were praying (Matthew 9:35-10:8). We pray because we see the fields ripening, so we must not be surprised when *we* are the workers Jesus calls: you and me. Don't be surprised if the one he sends is you. God has work for you to do, but first, you must open your eyes and see the need as Jesus does: the fields are ripe for harvest.

When we see lost souls as Jesus does, our motivation for service becomes the same as his: love for the Father. When we know who we were before we were saved, grateful love fuels our service. We are God's workmanship, created in Christ Jesus to do good works, and those works originate in the Father, who graciously calls us to be his hands and feet.

God has done many works in us and for us. He loved us, quickened us to new life, exalted us, and keeps us eternally secure. But God also has work for us to do. The works we were created to accomplish do not earn our salvation, but are the natural outflow of our salvation. Our deeds for the Lord proceed from a heart filled with love and gratitude. We *want* to be a part of the harvest because *we* have been harvested and received God's grace.

Fortunately for you and me, believers who came before us loved the Lord and desired to serve him. It's quite possible that we were a distraction for them—we probably trespassed into their comfort zone. Yet, likely, we were not scorned, judged, treated impatiently, or turned away. God ignited someone, maybe multiple people, to share the gospel with you, and, eventually, you responded in faith. Knowing we are not worthy of the gospel of grace poured out on us brings a natural desire to live worthy of this great salvation.

Amazingly, as we serve those God brings to us, he uses those same people as his tools to train us, paring away whatever keeps us from being fruitful. The very people we minister to help refine and polish us, revealing God's majesty and glory in us. Look at the people whom God has brought before you. God hand-picked each of them and deftly held them as a precision tool in his mighty hand to shape you and help make you into Jesus' image.

I have experienced how God intricately weaves lives together, using iron to sharpen iron. For years, I mentored teen moms, doing my best to lead them to the Lord. My heart desired that those precious young women would trust God to meet their needs: physical, emotional, spiritual, financial, and in every other realm. Amazingly, God used each of those beautiful ladies to teach me much about himself, the world, myself, and my place in the world. God used them to minister to me—changing, refining, and stretching me as he continued to work to mold me into the image of Jesus.

Sometimes, those I mentored were big distractions to my comfortable life. Phone calls came at all hours, and tears often didn't stop before our time together was scheduled to end. To say it wasn't always convenient is an understatement; their crises cropped up at the worst possible times, even as I cared for my own family.

Because all of my teen moms had to eat, and so did I, I tried to schedule our mentoring sessions over lunch and left my door open for drop-ins during the lunch hour. One teen who attended the local community college near me knew I'd almost always have something in the fridge for her and her toddler. Was she invading my space? Yes. Did she interrupt my quiet house and my work? Most certainly. Did she work her way deep into my heart? Absolutely. Did she pull me out of my comfort zone exponentially? Definitely. Did God use her to change my vision? Thankfully, yes. Was

I blessed beyond belief? Immeasurably. At my kitchen table, I had the privilege of introducing this sweet teenager to Jesus, the One who would become her Savior and her Lord, and not only hers but also her daughter's. The cycle of drug abuse, pre-marital sex, and single motherhood was broken. I didn't break it. Jesus did. Only Jesus can.

Jesus hones our vision so that we can see others as he sees them, and he sharpens our vision so that as we look inward, we can see ourselves as he sees us. We must learn to think of ourselves rightly. God's Word says no one should *think of himself more highly than he ought to think, but to think with sober judgment, each according to the measure of faith God has assigned* (Romans 12:3).

We must see ourselves honestly, with all our warts, bruises, wounds, scars, and shortcomings. We must see ourselves as unworthy of the grace we have received. The apostle Paul always retained the vision of himself as Saul, an undeserving recipient of grace. He knew who he was apart from God's grace and who he would have remained without God's grace. Paul was indebted to God's grace; therefore, his love for the Father fed his soul. Through the power of the Holy Spirit, Paul never ran out of something to give anyone who crossed his path because he never took Christ's grace for granted. And neither should we.

Compassion is an outflowing of grace. We will grow in our compassion when we recognize our unworthiness and all we have received. We will desire to see God minister to others in their brokenness and unworthiness, just as we know he has ministered to us.

Realizing that all we are, all we have, and all we ever will be is a gift of grace that comes from the heart of God gives us a proper view of ourselves and enables us to see an accurate image of others. Only as we perceive our own and others' needs correctly will we be able to discern the true solution, which is always Jesus. If we cannot see the need for Jesus' presence, then we are not looking at the problem correctly. We must trust Jesus to help us comprehend the problem and develop the compassion—that deep-seated sharing in another's suffering—that we need.

Look at the people around you. Oswald Chambers tells us that if we want to see ourselves as the Lord sees us, as the kind of people we are to God, we should look at the people he brings around us. So, look around; who do you see? The Twelve saw hungry people coming toward them, people who wanted Jesus' power in their physical lives but were unaware they needed him in their spiritual lives. Were the Twelve different from the crowd? Did they want Jesus' power personally? They wanted to be conduits of power, but did they sincerely want to be changed by his power? The Twelve felt spiritually full; they'd had a great victory just days before, yet they could not see clearly. Jesus used the multitude to train the Twelve to see as he sees.

As you lead others to Jesus, God is leading you. We can only lead as far as we have gone. As we serve others, we must first allow Jesus to serve us. We can only serve as much as we've been served. Jesus saw the crowd and felt compassion for the people and the Twelve. They had much to learn, and Jesus was ready to teach them. Jesus would not only meet the needs of the multitude but also the needs of the Twelve, teaching them that he meets our needs as we serve others.

To be his hands and feet, Jesus does not demand our perfect sanctification. He does not require that all our hurts be healed, all our emotional ducks be in a row, all our bad habits cleaned up, and all our weaknesses removed before he can use us. Just as he used the imperfect Twelve to serve the crowd, he will use us to serve others, just as we are. Do you need to ask God to give you a clear vision of your heart? Is it time to pray, *Search me, O God, and know my heart! Try me and know my thoughts! And see if there be any grievous way in me* (Psalm 139:23-24)? When God does illuminate your sin, confess it and repent of it. By doing so, Jesus will hone your vision, allowing you to see others more clearly and serve him in a more mighty way.

We must spend time with Jesus, allowing him to develop his vision in us. As our sight becomes clearer, our leadership for him will become increasingly more effective. We must see as Jesus sees and recognize that people need Jesus more than they need anything else, including us. The need for Jesus is a need for something eternal; any temporal or earthly fix will soon wear out or run out. If we want to serve, lead, or feed Jesus' sheep without starving ourselves to death, we must bring eternal food: Jesus, the Bread of Life. Only then can we be the hands and feet of Jesus, equipped to change the world.

Our call is not to win people to our way of thinking but to bring them the love of Jesus. We can only do that when we see people as Jesus sees them.

To become godly leaders who feed Jesus' sheep with compassion, **we must work with Jesus to hone our vision**. *We must repent of our shortsighted worldview and trust God to develop in us a worldview based on his Word; then, we will overcome spiritual shortsightedness and be better equipped to serve as competent workers.*

Questions for Discussion

1. Do you struggle to see people as Jesus sees them? When you see people in need, do you see hungry, hurting, and lost sheep? Or do you see distractions? Interruptions? Inconveniences?

2. What were your motives for first coming to Christ?

3. Do you see yourself as a recipient of grace or deserving of salvation?

4. Are you content to be a backup singer for Jesus?

5. Describe when you, like Moses or Paul, needed your vision honed.

6. How is Jesus using your service to accomplish your spiritual growth? As a polishing cloth? As sandpaper? As a refining fire?

7. Who is a distraction, keeping you from doing for Jesus what you want to do? What would need to change so that you no longer see them as distractions but as people who need Jesus?

8. Do you let others' obviously wrong motives keep you from serving them?

9. If everyone is constantly training someone, how are you training others, and how are they training you?

10. How are you most likely to react to distractions? With judgment? With impatience? With frustration? With aloofness?

11. Would you describe yourself as compassionate? Why or why not?

Chapter 4

Expect Tests

Count it all joy, my brothers, when you meet trials of various kinds, for you know that the testing of your faith produces steadfastness. And let steadfastness have its full effect, that you may be perfect and complete, lacking in nothing.
James 1:2-4

Have you ever dreamed that you're back in high school, about to take an exam, but you don't recall attending the class? It is a nightmare to feel so utterly unprepared. Although this is common, fortunately, it is just a dream. In real life, we usually attend class, and the teacher prepares us for the tests. However, when testing time arrives, the teacher is quiet. It is the teacher's—and our—time to discover what we've learned or failed to learn.

For us as Christians, there will also be tests; we can be sure of it. And, for the most part, it may seem like God is quiet while we are going through them. It helps to remember that our lives are the classroom, we have attended the training, and our Teacher is present in the test with us. While God may seem silent or distant during our times of testing, we know he has prepared us. God grows our faith through our circumstances, trials, sufferings, and joys, and then he tests that new growth, just as Jesus tested the faith of the Twelve.

Jesus had been with the disciples long enough to teach them much about himself. They experienced his power in their lives and ministries, saw him accomplish the miraculous, and heard him teach with authority. And then, there was a test of faith to reveal upon what or whom they placed their faith. *Lifting up his eyes, then, and seeing that a large crowd was coming toward him, Jesus said to Philip, "Where are we to buy bread, so that these people may eat?" He said this to test him, for he himself knew what he would do* (John 6:5-6).

Jesus, God the Son, the Second Person of the Trinity, knows everything, and because he is all-wise, he knows how best to apply that knowledge to bring about the best outcome. Therefore, we are assured that this predicament did not catch Jesus off guard, nor did it catch him without a plan. In every crisis, every difficulty, and every seemingly overwhelming and impossible situation, Jesus already knows what he will do. The test for godly leaders is to remember who Jesus is and to rely upon his character in all things. If the object of our faith is Jesus, when we find ourselves pressed to devise a plan, our plan will center on Jesus. That is the test. If our plans do not center on Jesus, they are not good plans, and we reveal that we have much to learn.

Through every detail of our lives, including our service to others, God teaches us to rely fully on him as we walk by faith. Even our relationship with Jesus is built on faith. Faith is what we believe—and faith must have an object. In what or whom do you place your faith, your belief? God's tests reveal whether Jesus is the object of our faith or if we have come to rely on and put our hope in anything or anyone else. Like the Twelve, we must learn that if we are to lead, serve, or minister to God's children, our faith must not be in our ability, experience, resources, or even in faith itself; our faith must be in Jesus alone.

The disciples planned to send the people away; they knew they didn't have what was needed to provide for the crowd. They had no faith in themselves or their ability. It is good, perhaps wise even, to know one's limitations, but it is not wise to leave Jesus out of the equation. The Twelve decided there was no point in trying if they couldn't meet the crowd's needs. If there were insufficient resources, why start what they knew they could not finish? Philip, quick to do the math, concluded that there was not enough money to purchase food for the crowd, nor was there time to earn enough money.

The disciples' first reaction was to follow their impulse: panic. The crowd was tremendous, they were few, and their resources were minimal (remember, they had not eaten yet; maybe they were a little hangry). The committee's consensus was solid: Send the crowd away. It only made sense to let the people fend for themselves. This was not a good plan. When any potential solution to any problem excludes Almighty God, we plan foolishly.

We Are Never Alone During the Test

We must remember who asked the Twelve, *"Where are we to buy bread?"* (John 6:5). Jesus asked the questions. Jesus was in control. It was Jesus, the One about whom God declared, *"You are my beloved Son; with you I am well pleased"* (Mark 1:11). It was Jesus, the hungry One, who withstood the temptations of the devil to turn stones into bread after forty days in the desert. Jesus, the One who saw Philip under the fig tree. Jesus, the One who turned water into wine at a wedding in Cana. Jesus, the One who cleared the Temple with authority. Jesus, the One who healed the official's son with his word. Jesus, the One who healed the lame man, the paralyzed man, the deformed man, the blind man, the mute man, and the people with leprosy. Jesus, the One who cast out demons. Jesus, the One who had authority over the fish in the sea and raised the widow's son and Jairus' daughter to life. Jesus, the One who calmed the storms and walked on water.

There was much Jesus taught the Twelve about who he was, but what had they learned? What did they have yet to learn about who they were, who they were not, and in whom they must always place their faith? The Gospels record that the Twelve were unanimous in their solution to send the people away to get food for themselves. Jesus was training them to let go of their self-reliance and rely on him for every problem, especially the unsolvable ones.

For the most part, we are capable men and women and can find ways to cope with the most challenging situations. However, we are not all-knowing, we are not all-wise, and we are not all-powerful. There is much we can do in many cases, and God expects us to use our wisdom, resources, and common sense, but we will never have sufficient resources to solve every problem. Even if we did, we may need to learn how to apply those resources for the best remedy. If we think we have sufficient resources, it is typically because of our limited vision; we don't know every facet of every problem or the consequences of even our best solutions.

More importantly, we do not know what Jesus will do. We do not know how he will use a particular set of circumstances to bring glory to himself. Therefore, we often only involve him once we get into an unfixable pickle. Or we ask him to rubber-stamp what we've done and bring success out of our potential failures.

We often think it is easier to tackle a dilemma alone than to involve God, ask his perspective, and implement his plan. On the flip side, if we can't figure out all the angles, all the what-ifs, or all the solutions, we might bail or pass the buck like the disciples did, thinking: The problem is too big; send them home. Fear of failure can cripple us. Self-reliance will stop us from experiencing God's mighty power at work. Limited wisdom deceives us into thinking less of God and more of ourselves.

Like the Twelve, we've spent time with Jesus; he's been teaching us, and we know some facts. We know that Jesus is eternal, and because he is eternal, he knows everything there is to know; he has all the knowledge there will ever be and knows how to dispense every resource for the best possible outcome. Yet, even though we have this head knowledge, we must experience it to understand it in our hearts. We must learn to see Jesus' involvement, knowledge, and wisdom in our daily personal issues. Espousing his attributes is easier if we've experienced them. For those unsure if you've experienced his involvement in your life, that begs the question: Why haven't you? Have you failed to ask him to get involved? If your salvation story is the most recent—or only—story you can recall of Jesus acting on your behalf, why is that?

At that moment, on that hillside, with thousands of hungry people facing him, Jesus didn't see a problem; he saw an opportunity to engage the disciples and meet the people's needs. So, Jesus asked the question. The test began, and then Jesus listened.

Even today, he asks us questions about our leadership, ministry, or service: How will you get volunteers? Where are you going to find a venue? How are you going to finance this? How are you going to convince people that this is a good idea? Then, he listens as he waits for us to complete the test. Jesus is never in a hurry to teach us all that we need to learn, and he is never in a hurry as he waits on us to demonstrate what we've learned; he has all eternity on his side, and there is no clock ticking. Oh, that we would slow down and enjoy his classroom while we are here. I imagine the Twelve still cringe when they think back to their first plan: Send them away. There is no glory in sending away those God has brought you to serve. We can be assured, however, that when God is involved, the supernatural will be accomplished and God alone will be glorified.

Tests Are Opportunities for Faith to Grow

This test was designed uniquely for the disciples for that day and moment. With his question, *"Where are we to buy bread, so that these people might eat?"* Jesus forced the Twelve to face facts. Fact One: There was no place to buy bread. Fact Two: There was no money with which to buy the bread. Fact Three: There were over five thousand hungry people to feed. Fact Four: It was getting late. Fact Five: This was too big a problem for the Twelve to resolve.

Despite knowing these facts, the Twelve overlooked the most significant fact: Jesus was in their midst. Jesus, who is God. Jesus, the One through whom all things were created (John 1:1-3), the all-sufficient Lord of all, the One who knew exactly what he was going to do. There was no need to panic. The Twelve had yet to learn that they had every reason to trust that Jesus would bring them through this impossible ordeal because Jesus had brought them to it. We must learn this lesson as well. We must repent of our self-reliance and rely on Jesus, the One worthy of our faith. If he has brought us to a problematic situation, he will see us through it.

When the task seems overwhelming (and this one sure did for the Twelve!), do we turn to Jesus and trust him to provide, or do we declare the situation beyond our ability? Do we seek excuses? I can't speak in public (neither could Moses). I'm too young (so were Jeremiah and Timothy). I'm not ready for a lifetime commitment (was Isaiah? Was Paul?). I don't know anyone there (did Ruth?). I can't leave here if I don't know where I'm going (what about Abraham?). I'm the runt, the least, the overlooked one in the family (so was David).

We all know those in the Bible are super-believers. No one expects regular Christians to do what they did. The heroes of the faith are unique; we are not like them. Right? Wrong! Those people were as ordinary as we are; they were just like us and had the same God we have. When their faith was tested, they persevered. What enabled them to stand firm in their tests? I suggest it was the object of their faith. They knew God, they believed him, and they trusted him completely.

These faithful believers held an amazingly high view of God; their faith was in his Word, character, and promises. They trusted God and placed their faith in him because they fully believed God was precisely who he said he was and was capable of doing what he said he would do. Their faith enabled them to step out and do what God asked them to do because their faith was not in their *idea* of God but in the *reality* of God. They understood God, his name, and his attributes. They knew that God was omniscient, omnipresent, and omnipotent. They lived their lives trusting in his promises, even though they did not see the fulfillment of those promises. God's Word tells us the world was not worthy of them. *They went about in skins of sheep and goats, destitute, afflicted, mistreated—of whom the world was not worthy—wandering about in deserts and mountains, and in dens and caves of the earth. And all these, though commended through their faith, did not receive what was promised* (Hebrews 11:37-40). The heroes of the Bible looked beyond their faith to the completeness of the Almighty, which is where our faith must also land.

When Jesus first looked out on the crowd and was stirred with compassion, he knew that if he took the time to teach and heal them, it would soon be mealtime, and they would all need to be fed. He could have stopped at any time and sent the people home. He didn't. He had a plan, and he invited the Twelve into it. How exciting it is to have a role in Jesus' plans!

When Jesus has a plan, we should get on board quickly and defer our strategies to his. We may often think he will ask, or has asked, more of us than we can handle. Likely, the twelve men who had no food and were suddenly responsible for feeding five thousand people felt that way. They could have said no. They could have debated with Jesus. Yet, they knew that belaboring their inability or failing to recognize Jesus' ability would slander him and make a mockery of who he was. My inability to accomplish a task doesn't negate my availability to work for God; it enhances his ability to work through me. My inability is God's opportunity to reveal his strength. *But he said to me, "My grace is sufficient for you, for my power is made perfect in weakness." Therefore I will boast all the more gladly about my weaknesses, so that the power of Christ may rest upon me. For the sake of Christ, then, I am content with weaknesses, insults, hardships, persecutions, and calamities. For when I am weak, then I am strong* (2 Corinthians 12:9-10). *I can do all things through him [Christ] who strengthens me* (Philippians 4:13). *"I am the vine; you are the branches. Whoever abides in me and I in him, he it is that bears much fruit, for apart from me you can do nothing"* (John 15:5).

The Twelve could have fed all those people if there had been a substantial stash of cash, a readily available burger joint, or a pizza delivery guy nearby. However, who then would have received the glory? The praise? The adulation and thanksgiving? When we rely solely on our resources, experience, and capabilities, how does our plan bring glory to God? When we fail to engage God in our projects, we fail to serve as God would have us serve. Would anyone see God at work if the Twelve possessed all the resources necessary to feed this multitude? No, because God would not have been at work; the Twelve would have been.

It is wrong to hold back from starting or completing a task that God has called us to if we do not engage because we feel incapable or can't fathom an outcome. It is inappropriate to complain about what we don't have. When we cannot see where to begin or how to move forward, we must rely on what we know to be true: When God calls us to a specific work, he will see us through. God can do all that he says he will do, and when he involves us in his plan, he will surely do mighty work in us and through us in such a way that he receives all the glory. In other words, he will do that which we could never do apart from him.

When God calls us to engage in a problem, situation, ministry, or program where we feel out of control or uncomfortably insufficient, we can trust that is precisely where we need to be to learn to rely on him. Yet even the apostle Paul, who operated entirely in God's perfect will, doing what God called him to do, had difficulty. He wrote, *For we do not want you to be unaware, brothers, of the affliction we experienced in Asia. For we were so utterly burdened beyond our strength that we despaired of life itself. Indeed, we felt that we had received the sentence of death. But that was to make us rely not on ourselves but on God who raises the dead* (2 Corinthians 1:8-9). When we are in God's service, things are sometimes hard to endure.

Some people like to say that God will never give us more than we can handle. Unfortunately, that is not true. God often allows or gives us more than we can handle; otherwise, we would not need to rely on or exercise our faith in him. If we could handle all of life, we would not see a need for God. We may wonder if God is testing us when he calls us to a service beyond our ability. Is he training us to rely on him? We don't know how our difficult situations will end, but we know we have a trustworthy God who has placed us or allowed us to land smack in the middle of them. If we fail to begin or follow through with a task because it feels overwhelming or our available resources are small, we will forfeit seeing God work, and maybe even provide a bountiful ending.

Tests Prove the Trustworthiness of Our Faith

Jesus was training the Twelve to look to and rely on him. He was teaching them to trust him and recognize that, while they were insufficient, he was more than sufficient. He was training them to remain calm in the face of extraordinary challenges and to evaluate themselves honestly in light of their ministry and faith.

We know we can't do everything, but that doesn't mean we should not accept a call or persevere in a call to service simply because we don't have all the answers. Sometimes, we don't even have the right questions. Our questions often hinge on circumstances we can see when the answers can only be found in things that cannot be seen: the faith God has given us.

As we ask the necessary questions, we might find that the answers include two truths: 1) Accomplishing what we are called to is impossible without Jesus. 2) Accomplishing what we are called to is possible only with Jesus. Because God's plan involves us each actively participating in service—the purpose we were created for—we must serve in faith. However, we were not designed to go it alone. We all have gifts that complement one another, and each person's gift is of equal value in the church's edification. *For as in one body we have many members, and the members do not all have the same function, so we, though many, are one body in Christ, and individually members one of another. Having gifts that differ according to the grace given to us, let us use them* (Romans 12:4-6a).

Using the gifts God has lavished upon us is an exercise of faith. We should never hoard our gifts nor fear their insufficiency. God knows every detail of every need and provides for those needs perfectly. When we fail to use our gifts generously, the church—and the projects to which God calls us—suffer. God has every resource in the universe at his disposal and abundantly dispenses gifts and talents to his people. Therefore, when we are tested, we should recognize the test as an opportunity to rely on him and use what he has given us.

I recall a time when I invited a woman into a leadership position in a Bible study. She was gifted and equipped to lead, but her elementary-school-aged children needed to catch the school bus at the exact same time she needed to be at the church. She and I prayed together, and we both believed that God had called her into this place of leadership. Yet, there was no way that she could get to the church on time if she had to wait for the bus to pick up her children, and there was no neighbor to watch her children on those mornings. So, she made the best decision she could think of in light of the facts she could see: she offered to resign.

I could have let her walk away; it appeared impossible for her to step into this service role. Instead, I reminded her that we had prayed through this, and both earnestly believed God had called her to this ministry.

I asked again, "Do you believe God called you to this ministry?"

"Yes."

"Do you believe God will equip you to do what he has asked?"

"Yes."

"Have you exhausted every possibility for your children's transportation?"

"Yes."

There was only one thing to do: ask God for a miracle and then wait. This was a test of faith for both of us. We had no resources to fall back on, and neither of us was gifted in driving school buses.

The Bible study was scheduled to begin the day after the Labor Day holiday, which was also the first day of school. If this woman could not make it, many women would be placed on a waiting list until a new leader could be secured and trained. My friend didn't want to leave me in a bind, so on the Friday before Labor Day, she called me and said that it didn't look like she would be able to meet the schedule, so again, she offered to resign. We had the same conversation, prayed, and exercised the same faith. I was vacationing in a very remote area with limited cell phone coverage; whenever I could, I checked my phone, but there were no missed calls. I kept praying and waiting.

In the final hours of that holiday weekend, she received notification that the bus schedule had changed. What?! God miraculously acted on her behalf! A friend told her that the bus route had not changed since its inception years before, yet it changed for my friend. And the decision was made on a holiday weekend. Do school administrators regularly work on holiday weekends? They did that year. Had they ever changed a bus route the day before school started? They did that year. Our inability to effect changes on our own is glaringly apparent. We cannot accomplish God's work apart from him. Yet, when God is involved, all things are possible! This was a test of faith. We trusted God, and God did what he said he'd do. He called her to service and equipped her to do it by taking care of her children's transportation. When Jesus involves us in his work, he is also at work in our circumstances.

Jesus involved the Twelve in his plan when he asked them, *"Where are we to buy bread?"* Jesus sent out the Twelve on their previous mission with his authority over the spiritual realm, and now he tested them regarding the material; they worried that they had no food or money. Tests are designed to reveal our faith or lack thereof because faith that is not tested is faith that cannot be trusted. The Twelve had placed their faith in Jesus, and Jesus tested that faith: Would they trust him with the unknown? Would they wait on him? Would they turn to him for help? Would they do whatever he asked?

Our faith must also be tested to know whether it will withstand life's stress, heartaches, and pressures. When we first come to faith, we are like kindergarteners; our enthusiasm and passion for God are exuberant. Yet, our faith is immature because our knowledge of God is immature. We know and love Jesus, but do we trust that he will sustain us through trials, difficulties, heartache, and despair? Through our suffering, as we experience God's all-sufficient grace and character, our faith matures and enables us to move into the next classroom. Those tests teach us that we can rely on God's faithfulness. As each challenge of faith produces a new level of trust, God must test our deeper faith to show us where we have grown and to reveal how strong that developing faith has become. His tests also reveal whether our faith is in anything other than God. Do we trust him to be sufficient in our insufficiency? Do we trust him to be strong in our weakness? Do we trust him to give us the wisdom we seek? Do we trust him to lead us day by day along new paths? Do we trust him to equip us in every arena for whatever work he calls us to?

The Twelve experienced a tremendous growth spurt on their earlier mission trip. They had experienced a new level of faith in Jesus as they relied on his equipping and authority. They trusted his authority over unclean spirits, and they trusted his provision. And now, this new level of faith had to be tested. Was it as strong as they thought? Would it hold? Would they surrender their self-reliance and trust Jesus? Or would they walk away?

Tests reveal the object of our faith. In what had the Twelve placed their faith? The test would reveal whether it was their success, their ability, or Jesus. It could reveal a truth that they would prefer not to be told. Consider that only a few moments before, they were rejoicing that the evil spirits submitted to them, and now their success hinged on five thousand hungry people and a lack of money, with no time to earn any. It seemed their only choice was to send the people away.

If we are to serve boldly and confidently, without bailing or turning tail and running, our faith must rest in the Lord Jesus Christ. But what, exactly, is faith? Faith is belief. We believe in something, and we act on that belief. Faith that saves us has three components: a mental assent to the facts, a warming response of the heart, and a commitment to live for Christ.

First: Faith is a mental assent to the facts. The facts we must know and believe are the facts that God has given to us in his Word. We must understand who Jesus is: He is both fully human and fully God. He came to earth, lived a perfectly human, sinless life, died on the cross in our place (as our substitute), was resurrected on the third day, and lives exalted in heaven. *Who, though he was in the form of God, did not count equality with God a thing to be grasped, but emptied himself, by taking the form of a servant, being born in the likeness of men. And being found in human form, he humbled himself by becoming obedient to the point of death, even death on a cross. Therefore God has highly exalted him and bestowed on him the name that is above every name, so that at the name of Jesus every knee should bow, in heaven and on earth and under the earth, and every tongue confess that Jesus Christ is Lord, to the glory of God the Father* (Philippians 2:6-11).

The second component of faith is a warming response of the heart. We must experience an inner drawing of God and an emotional connection to those facts. There must be a rending of the heart that results in a response of love to God, who first loved us and sent his only Son as our atoning rescue. Before faith becomes real to us, there must be brokenness in the soul; otherwise, we will never see the need for a Savior. *Falling to the ground, he heard a voice saying to him, "Saul, Saul, why are you persecuting me?" And he said, "Who are you, Lord?" and he said, "I am Jesus, whom you are persecuting"* (Acts 9:4-5).

Finally, the third component of faith is a commitment to live for Christ Jesus. We surrender our will and vow to live for and follow Christ. He becomes more than our example; he becomes our Lord. *"Truly, truly I say to you, unless a grain of wheat falls into the earth and dies, it remains alone; but if it dies, it bears much fruit. Whoever loves his life loses it, and whoever hates his life in this world will keep it for eternal life. If anyone serves me, he must follow me"* (John 12:24-26a).

The test of genuine saving faith is whether we are willing to trust Jesus alone to save us or feel we need to add to his saving grace. The proof of that choice is laying down our lives daily and picking up our cross. What does that mean? What does it look like? Our cross is where our will, desires, and plans for ourselves intersect with God's will, desires, and plans for us. Those intersections are where God asks us if we will lay down our self-sufficiency and trust his sufficiency. At those intersections, we willingly submit to God's more excellent plans, knowing that they are always best for us, and lay down our will, desires, and plans that contradict his.

The Twelve were learning to trust Jesus' authority, wisdom, and plans. Jesus asked, *"Where are we to buy bread?"* There was no place to buy bread. And there was no money. Difficult situations are classrooms where opportunities for faith to grow and mature abound. We must learn that when we are at the end of ourselves, at the end of our resources, and at the end of our ability, God is there waiting to act. The test is almost always: Will you trust God to be who he says he is and do what he says he will do?

To become godly leaders who feed Jesus' sheep with confidence, we must **learn to expect tests** *and embrace them. We must repent of self-sufficiency, fear, anxiety, and whatever else threatens to prevent us from trusting God, and stand firm in the test as we stand on the foundation of Jesus.*

Questions for Discussion

1. In whom or what have you placed your faith?

2. In what or whom are you most tempted to place your faith? Your personality? Your planning? Your resources? Your organizational skills? Your pastor? Your church? Your co-workers? Your program?

3. How is God currently testing your faith?

4. What problems are you facing that seem impossible to solve?

5. What attributes of God do you find the most trustworthy? What qualities do you struggle to trust? Why?

6. Which seems more natural to you: relying on yourself or relying on God? Why?

7. Are you honestly evaluating yourself? What gifts or talents has God given you? How are you using them to edify the body of Christ?

8. What have your tests of faith revealed about your relationship with God?

9. Are you serving where God has uniquely equipped you to serve?

10. When you feel tempted to give up or give in, how does the knowledge that God is with you in the test enable you to persevere?

Chapter 5

Nothing Is Too Wonderful for God

"Behold, like the clay in the potter's hand, so are you in my hand."
Jeremiah 18:6b

Taking on the impossible, where failure seems apparent, has not typically been my idea of how to serve God's people. I lean toward a program with a well-thought-out plan, a staff anxious to accomplish the task, and measurable goals. But God has the sovereign authority to call us to any service at any time in any place, even if we cannot see how that service can be accomplished. That's when we get a front-row seat to watch Jesus at work. Maybe that's why Jesus sometimes asks us to join him in the impossible.

When asked to do the impossible, to serve in a way we never imagined or planned for, every bit of confidence rooted in our talent, resources, education, wisdom, and self-reliance flies out the window. When things are possible, we focus on the possibilities. Who wouldn't be willing to jump in and do that which we know has a high probability of success? That's an easy path to victory. It guarantees a pat on the back and foretells a promotion. Yet, how much more challenging and exciting is it to be asked to participate in the impossible?

Jesus invited the Twelve into the impossible with one quick command: *"You give them something to eat"* (Matthew 14:16). How could they? They were as hungry and as impoverished as the people they were commanded to serve. The Twelve had nothing. Perhaps this is the exact reason Jesus told them to feed the multitude. As Oswald Chambers said, "The knowledge of our own poverty is what brings us to the proper place where Jesus Christ accomplishes his work."[1] These ordinary men would quickly understand the poverty of their circumstances, both materially and spiritually. *But Jesus said, "They need not go away; you give them something to eat"* (Matthew 14:16).

Wait. What? Give them something to eat? Who said that? Are you kidding me? Give them something to eat? There's nothing here. There's no money. There's no time to earn money. There's no way. Do you know what you are asking us to do? You are asking too much.

Have you ever had similar thoughts? I assume you and I would have if we had been standing with the Twelve, because these are everyday thoughts for ordinary people. Nevertheless, none of us has the right to question Jesus' right or his authority to command us to do anything at any time, even though we've been known to do just that.

Are we prone to question Jesus' commands and challenge his authority when it involves the seemingly impossible (like forgiving someone who has offended us, loving our enemies, submitting to authority, respecting our government when we disagree with it, or honoring our parents)? Our pathetic challenges do not negate the truth that Jesus has every right to command whatever he desires of us. He has that right because he is our Lord. Jesus knew what he was doing when he told the Twelve to give the multitude something to eat.

---

1. Chambers, Oswald, *My Utmost For His Highest: Updated Edition*. Oswald Chambers Publications, Association Ltd, 1992. July 21

Jesus Has Every Right to Tell Us What to Do

Jesus has the right to tell us what to do because it was through him that we were made: *All things were made through him, and without him was not any thing made that was made* (John 1:3)—including us. He has the right to tell us what to do because he redeemed us: *Knowing that you were ransomed from the futile ways inherited from your forefathers, not with perishable things such as silver or gold, but with the precious blood of Christ, like that of a lamb without blemish or spot* (1 Peter 1:18-19). Jesus has the right to tell us what to do because he purchased us for God: *"You were slain, and by your blood you ransomed [purchased NIV] people for God from every tribe and language and people and nation"* (Revelation 5:9).

We have no right to dictate to the Lord what we will or will not do, nor to tell him what he can or cannot command us to do, because we are his servants. He has the authority as God; we are the pot, and he is the Potter, not vice versa. He created us, and he has sovereign dominion over us. The Lord can tell us to do that which seems impossible, and we have no right to balk. Yet, we do; and we doubt. We fear the impossible because it is, well, impossible! We don't want to fail or appear as failures. It requires humility to admit to God that we cannot do what he is asking, and it requires great faith to trust that he has a plan to accomplish the very service he is asking us to do.

We must remember that a servant obeys because the master commands; it doesn't matter what the command is. How much more we will want to submit because we have a Master who loves us and whom we love. Our Master—our Lord Jesus—promises never to leave nor forsake us, so we are not left to our own devices to accomplish what he has commanded us to do. We have no reason to fear what he asks us to do, no reason to fear stepping out in obedience, and no reason to think we must rely solely on our pitiful resources. The One who loves us most is walking with us. It is our privilege to step into the impossible with him.

I'm sure the Twelve were shocked when Jesus called them to the impossible task of feeding thousands. However, the Twelve didn't second-guess who spoke to them. Jesus was with them. They knew him. They knew his voice. You and I do not have Jesus standing physically before us, so we often question if he is the one calling us to serve, unsure of whose voice we are hearing: Jesus'? Our own? Someone else's?

When asked to do anything outside what we think is doable, we sometimes debate, asking, "Is this my calling?" Perhaps our concern and questions, even our debate, is the siren bell to come away with God and ask him personally, one-on-one, "Did you ask me to do this thing? Is this your call for me? What would you have me do?" Instead, how likely are we to gather our friends and ask them to pray for us to know what God would have us do? We listen to their opinions and input, becoming more confused or reinforced in our doubt or disobedience. Sometimes, rather than praying to ask God to confirm a call, we spend our time telling him why it is impossible, convincing ourselves that this is not a call from God. Can you imagine the Twelve going into a conference and asking each other to pray and ask God if Jesus had just told them to give the people something to eat?

The Twelve knew Jesus' voice, and so do we. As Christians, Jesus promises that *"the sheep follow him, for they know his voice. A stranger they will not follow"* (John 10:4b-5a). Sometimes, though, our desires, selfishness, perceived needs, and the cacophony of voices surrounding us can drown out the voice of our Shepherd, making it harder to distinguish his voice; so we must be intentional about listening to it and for it.

When asked to do any service for Jesus, we need to know positively that it is Jesus doing the asking; we must hear his voice. While some say they have heard an audible voice, I have never heard God speak to me that way. He talks to me through the pages of the Bible and in my heart, spirit, and thoughts; sometimes, it is so perceptible that it could almost be audible. However, that doesn't mean he won't or can't speak in an audible voice to me; it just means that this is how I have learned to hear my Shepherd's voice. Often, Jesus' call will come through another human being in the form of a request or a suggestion, but even then, when the call, text, or message arrives, if it is a call from Jesus, I know I will hear Jesus' voice of confirmation.

That said, how can we know with certainty if a phone call or a conversation is a call to service? First, know that God will never ask us to do something that contradicts his written Word. God doesn't change: *The sum of your word is truth, and every one of your righteous rules endures forever* (Psalm 119:160). God will not call you or me to something illegal or immoral; that is outside of his character. However, he may call us to do things entirely within our equipping, education, and desires or to do something beyond our comfort zone. Either way, that is his prerogative; he is God. Our responsibility is to be so in tune with God, through his Spirit, through studying his Word, and through living holy lives, that we know his good and perfect will for us. We train our ears to hear his voice as we spend time with him, study his Word, and obey each time he calls.

When God calls us to work, we do not have an option to decline; anything other than moving forward in faithfulness and trust is disobedience. But we're often so busy, with many people pulling us in different directions, that we may not see how to fit one more thing into our schedule. However, when we say "no," we stop listening to God, so we never hear exactly how he intended us to accomplish the calling. Though the mission may seem undoable, unrealistic, or ridiculous at the moment, we can trust that if God commissions us, there is a reason. We can rest assured that, despite how impossible or stretching a task may seem, God is purposeful, intent, and in control. And nothing is too wonderful for him. The Twelve had no idea how to solve this problem, but Jesus did; he always does. He knows how to solve ours, too. Nothing is too complicated for God.

How do we know that nothing is too hard for God? He's given us many illustrations in the Bible. For example, in John 11, when Jesus told Martha to take the stone away outside of Lazarus' tomb, Martha's thoughts were probably as skeptical as those the Twelve were thinking on that hillside: But, Lord, you can't be serious, can you? Do you know how bad the smell will be? Do you know that I will look foolish and be embarrassed in front of my friends? Do you know how much a dead body has decomposed in this heat? Do you want to expose all of these people to something so unclean? Do you know what you are telling me to do? It is too much to ask.

Those hypothetical concerns are worldly, and yet, we all have them. This is precisely what we would have said. Have we forgotten John's words: *This is the love of God, that we keep his commandments. And his commandments are not burdensome. For everyone who has been born of God overcomes the world. And this is the victory that has overcome the world—our faith* (1 John 5:3-4)? When we add our expectations, fears, predispositions, and the world's standards to God's commands, they become burdensome. Martha was tested when she was commanded to roll the stone away. Would she obey?

Did Jesus listen to her concerns? Yes. Did they sway him? No. Jesus reminded Martha that she would see God's glory if she believed. This was her moment of decision. Would she trust Jesus? Would she do the one thing he asked her to do—take the stone away? Indeed, hers was not an impossible task but an unlikely one that required setting aside her pride and worldly concerns and surrendering to Jesus' authority. Would she? Not knowing what Jesus would do, not knowing he would call her brother back from the dead, not knowing whether she would be humiliated or if she would lose everything—her position in the community, respect, ceremonial cleanness—would she trust Jesus and do the one thing he asked her to do?

Martha chose to obey Jesus: She took the stone away. Did it stink? Probably. Did people think she was foolish? Most likely. Did she see the glory of God? Absolutely! Martha was more concerned about doing what Jesus said, even if it made no sense, than she was about failing to maintain respectable customs before the watchful eyes of her friends, family, and neighbors. Her priorities were in alignment with God's. She knew the One who told her what to do. She loved him. She trusted him. So she obeyed. And she saw the glory of God most spectacularly: Her dead brother lived!

Unfortunately, many of us fear embarrassment before the world more than we fear failing to obey God. We'd rather not do anything than risk the public humiliation of failure. We don't want to appear unsuccessful, so to keep our public accounts in the black, we let our spiritual accounts dip into the red.

Jesus Does Not Rely on Our Sufficiency; We Are Reliant on His

When Jesus told the Twelve to feed the people, they responded (I paraphrase), "But Lord, are you serious? That would take more money than we could make in half a year. And even if we did have it, are you kidding? You'd want us to spend that much on bread to give each person one little meal? And then what? Seriously, Jesus, we can't do it. We don't have the resources, we don't have the time, we don't have the means, we can't be all things to all people, and we can't meet these people's needs. Send them away."

Should we think that Jesus didn't know more about the situation than the Twelve ever could? They didn't need to remind him of all they didn't have. Yes, they were poor, yet they were standing with the Lord of lords, the King of kings, the One who had authority over everything. The Twelve were anything but paupers when they were with Jesus, but it seems they had forgotten who he was.

When we hear the call to serve or persevere in service, we must remember who Jesus is and that he is with us. When we focus on our schedules, commitments, and desires, and begin debating with God, we, like the Twelve, can quickly feel overwhelmed. And like Martha, we may teeter on the edge of missing out on the glory of God. How can I do this? How could I possibly fit in one more thing? We may not voice the debate aloud, but it is there. It is there in our hesitation. It is there in our fear. It is there in our desire to turn and walk away.

Years ago, part of a weekly program that I led included a fellowship hour before class once a month. The class had not been participating in the fellowships for quite some time because the small group leaders had determined it was impossible for their group members, or themselves, to arrive at the church an hour earlier in the evening after working a full day, preparing dinner for their families, and then fighting traffic to get to the church. I knew the class members needed the opportunity to bond and get to know one another apart from the study, and they were missing out. Since it was a vital part of the program's design, as the class leader, I prayerfully decided to re-implement the fellowships.

During the training session, when I introduced the plan, there were more than a few eye-rolls, and one of the more senior leaders spoke up, saying, "You don't know what you're asking."

I assured her I did, then asked a few questions. "Do you believe this is God's program? Do you believe that the guideline to include monthly fellowships was prayed over, determined to be part of God's plan for this program, and then included in it? Do you believe you were called to be a leader in this program? If the answer to those questions is 'Yes,' then let's pray and ask God to equip us to serve the women as he has called us to serve."

After the meeting, one of the newer leaders lingered and privately explained, "This is physically impossible for me; I cannot get away from work early enough to make the trip to the church in that timeframe."

I asked her, "Do you believe this is God's program? Do you believe you were called as a leader? Doesn't it seem outside the character of God to ask you to do the impossible and then sit back and watch you fail? Let's pray; ask God to get you here and see what happens."

On the next class night, I intentionally arrived fifteen minutes before the fellowship hour—I was not going to be late. But I was not the first one to arrive at the church. My lingerer from our training session was waiting in the foyer when I walked through the door. She'd been there ten minutes. When I asked her if she had taken the afternoon off from work, she replied that a coworker suggested an alternate route when she mentioned the new schedule and the impossible expectations at work. The leader tried the new way and had no problem meeting the fellowship time.

God will never ask us to do something and then sit back and watch us fail. However, we *will* fail if we pridefully rely only on ourselves and refuse to submit to his authority. It is amazing what God will do in, for, and through us when we respond obediently to whatever he calls us to and then rely on his equipping to accomplish the task. God is so good to us!

It's always important to pray about a call to service before we accept it, but what exactly do we pray for? Praying for confirmation is terrific: "Is this my call?" Telling God why we can't do it is probably not the best way to pray. However, even worse is trying to convince God that he has the wrong guy or gal. Although we may find many excuses for not accepting a call, especially a service or a task that appears likely to fail or is more significant than anything we imagine ourselves doing, we rarely find a *reason* to refuse a call. There is quite a difference between an excuse and a reason.

Hopefully, we agree that Jesus has every right to tell us what to do and that he never makes mistakes, so we should want to accept every call. But, like the Twelve, sometimes God's call just seems to be too much. Why did Jesus tell the Twelve to feed the people when it was impossible? Is there another competency in which Jesus trained the Twelve, the multitudes, and perhaps you and me? Jesus' challenge to the Twelve brings as many questions as answers.

Godly Leaders Embrace Their Poverty

Jesus knew what he would do, but no one else did. Was Jesus humbling the Twelve? Encouraging them? Challenging them? To help us understand, let's return to the events just before this miracle. The Twelve were coming off a mission experience, rejoicing that they had healed many people and that even the demons had submitted to them. These were men who desired greatness; they had even argued about which of them was greatest (Luke 9:46). They had not eaten, and their time alone with Jesus was interrupted. Then they had watched as Jesus healed the sick and cast demons out of the oppressed until it began getting late. Everyone was tired and hungry; it was a potentially volatile moment as no food was available.

Was Jesus humiliating the Twelve? Was he revealing their powerlessness before the crowd? Was he doubly impressing upon them the reality that they couldn't possibly tend to the group despite their great success only days before? I've read that some think that is the case, but I'm not sure; that seems far outside of Jesus' personality. Isaiah prophesied that the Messiah would not break a bruised reed or snuff out a smoldering wick, but that the

Messiah, Jesus, would be an encourager. He would not frustrate the people by setting forth a standard or task that could not be attained or completed with his help. Nevertheless, the Twelve were experiencing an obstacle that they could not overcome—several thousand hungry souls and no means of feeding them.

Oswald Chambers says, "God allows us to expose our ignorance by stumbling over obstacles in our way."[2] Is there ignorance among the Twelve that needs exposing? What obstacle are they stumbling over? I submit that they have forgotten who Jesus is, and they are ignorantly oblivious to Jesus' ability to meet their needs. They were clueless about Jesus' thoughts and motives for telling them to feed the people, and most confusing is that no one asked him "Why?" or "With what?" or "What are you thinking?" or "How do you suggest we do that?" Why didn't the Twelve turn to Jesus and seek his input? Seek his plan? Seek his guidance? Why don't we?

"You feed them." I'm familiar with their response, more than familiar with the obstacle they are tripping over, and intimately familiar with the revealed ignorance. Therefore, I will call it out: Their obstacle was pride as they adopted the stance, "This is all up to me." When we trip over pride, we forget who Jesus is. We forget that he is there and he is in control. Every time we stumble over pride, we brilliantly display our ignorance of Jesus' limitless, mighty, incredible power. That is not a light we want to shine. We must continually submit to the fact that we are nothing and can do nothing apart from Jesus. Just as you and I must, the Twelve had to come to terms with not how poor they thought they were, but how poor they were apart from Jesus.

---

2. Chambers, Oswald, *My Utmost for His Highest: Updated Edition.* Oswald Chambers Publications, Ltd. 1992. July 21

We must all come to the place where we recognize how poor we are apart from Jesus. In the Sermon on the Mount, Jesus says, *"Blessed are the poor in spirit for theirs is the kingdom of heaven"* (Matthew 5:3); that means that to enter the kingdom of heaven, we must recognize that we are spiritually bankrupt. We have nothing with which to save ourselves and nothing with which to save others. Even though we have been saved by grace through faith in the Lord Jesus Christ, we must continually recognize that apart from Jesus, we still have nothing to give.

Those God calls us to serve will receive nothing from us as long as we pretend to have more than we do. To serve effectively, we must admit our poverty, which requires humility. We must admit to ourselves, others, and God that we have nothing apart from God. If we fail to approach our service or accept his call with any attitude other than humility and total reliance on him, we are already starving. We must repent of our pride and embrace true humility.

Humility is not thinking less of ourselves; it is thinking of ourselves less. Humility recognizes and accepts who we are and who we are not; it acknowledges we don't know everything and readily admits we know very little. Humility confesses we do not have all the answers or even know all the questions and concedes we are not indispensable, nor are we irreplaceable. Humility gratefully assents that God doesn't need us; he can do whatever he desires with or without us, but he graciously and mercifully chooses to use us to accomplish his purposes and plans. Humility praises God and thanks him for his grace in choosing us and allowing us to work for his kingdom and glory.

At the same time, humility does not degrade, deny, or discount our abilities, talents, and gifts, prompting us to think we are less than we are; that is false humility. You and I are made in the image of God, and as his children, we have been given much. If we look at ourselves and think that there's no way God would ever use us or that we are completely ineffective in our service, that is false humility. Using our humility as an excuse for not getting involved in God's program is false humility. And false humility is pride.

In his Romans commentary, James Montgomery Boice says it best, "The second error in our evaluation of ourselves is to think too lowly of ourselves and so exude a false kind of humility. Sometimes this is really pride, because when we tell people bad things about ourselves what we really want them to say is, 'No, I don't think you're like that at all. I think you're really intelligent' (or wise or attractive or kind or whatever.) 'That helps,' we say. 'Keep it up. Tell me more. I'd like you to talk me out of this.' When we act like that, we are really being proud rather than humble, and we show it at once if the other person agrees with our earlier negative self-evaluation. We're offended when a friend says, 'Yes, I guess you really are stupid' (or ugly or ineffective or a hopeless case.)"[3]

Pride manifests itself in more ways than we can imagine, such as when we rush full speed ahead trying to accomplish the impossible on our own, fail to begin because we fear failure, or make excuses because of our perceived insignificance. Humility, on the other hand, tells us we need to stay in step with God and not worry about the outcome, and that we are more than significant because we are sons and daughters of the King.

"You give them something to eat." There's nothing to give. There's no place to get anything. There's no money with which to buy anything if there were anything to get. If the people are to receive anything, it must come from Jesus. Pride must be set aside, a humble acknowledgment of poverty must be adopted, and faith and trust in God's authority and

---

3. Boice, James Montgomery, *Romans, Vol 4, The New Humanity Romans 12-16*. Baker Books. 1995. Pg. 1568

provision must be exercised. This is true not only for the Twelve during this event in history, but it is necessary for each of us in every circumstance. Nothing is too difficult for God, and pretty much everything is impossible without him. Humbling? Yes. True? Absolutely.

Jesus was training the Twelve in humility—to look to him and trust him completely. He was also teaching them to be grateful. They had nothing. They had no plan, yet God was calling them to service. "You give them something to eat." Perhaps that is the most fantastic call to service—when we are commissioned to do something beyond our capabilities, we must rely entirely on whatever God gives, however much or little. We must learn to be grateful for the opportunity to serve and thankful in advance for the equipping. God will *equip you with everything good that you may do his will* (Hebrews 13:21a).

Once we recognize the voice of our Great Shepherd beckoning us to take action, we must step out in faith, accept the call, and persevere through the task, even in the face of the impossible. We must trust him to provide everything we need to accomplish all he has asked us to do. He will equip us. He will supply us with time, energy, resources, and emotional, physical, and mental strength. He will give us all that is required for us to fulfill his calling. This remarkable historical event illustrates that when a miracle is necessary, God will come through. However, as he provides, God alone has the authority and the wisdom to decide what the miracle will look like. A miracle is a blessing that comes only from God; when he calls us to do the seemingly impossible, he will provide the miracle to make it happen—even if it is as simple as a suggestion by a coworker to try a different route.

Do we forfeit miracles because we fail to come before God and humbly ask him for help? Would we see more miracles if we stopped stumbling over our pride? Could we feed more of Jesus' sheep if we stopped trying to do things on our own, in our way, relying only upon what we have?

Everything is impossible if we only focus on what we can see. God is the God of the impossible; nothing is too extraordinary for him. If we could meet every need we see, we wouldn't need God.

Thankfully, God does not depend on our self-reliance. Because God is good, we know he would not tell us to do something that he did not intend for our good or for the good of those we serve. Nor would he prevent us from serving as we rely on him, which seems to go against his character. And because he is trustworthy, we have no reason not to trust him to provide everything we need. Nevertheless, we are often much like the boy's father, who came to Jesus for healing: We believe, but we need help overcoming our unbelief (Mark 9:24). God can, but will he?

We believe God will provide; we just aren't sure exactly how, when, or to what degree. We fear that God's provision will not meet our standards. Are we, therefore, hesitant to accept a call when we can't see what the future holds, afraid that God will not come through and leave us falling short? God planned to feed the crowd, not just give them a bite. But the Twelve didn't know and couldn't see that.

Because our perspective is biased, we ask God for what we need based only on what we can see. God's provision, however, is unbiased; he gives what he knows we need. So when God doesn't provide exactly what we've asked him for, we have to learn to trust in his perfection. Just as God provided the exact amount of manna for the Israelites in the desert every day for forty years, we can trust God to supply exactly what we need for today. God's timing and provision are always perfect. Lord, we believe; please help us overcome our unbelief.

Jesus fully trusted God to furnish everything he needed. He never worried, never panicked, and never questioned God's provision. Jesus lived humbly and trusted the Father's faithfulness. Because Jesus knew his own identity—that he had come from God and was returning to God—he did all things humbly. *Jesus, knowing that the Father had given all things into his hands, and that he had come from God and was going back to God, rose from supper. He laid aside his outer garments, and taking a towel, tied it around his waist. Then he poured water into a basin and began to wash the disciples' feet and to wipe them with the towel that was wrapped around him* (John 13:3-5).

When we know who and whose we are, there is no room—or need—for pride. When we know that we belong to the Creator of all things, we are not afraid to do whatever he asks or tells us. We are not scared to face the impossible because we know that Jesus is always with us and has authority over everything, even the impossible. We do not fear failure because we trust God's definition of success, and we know God will not abandon us. Choosing to live humbly means trusting the Father and obeying his commands, just like Jesus did.

We grow in humility and meekness as we grasp the truth of who we are in Christ. We embrace our poverty apart from him and admit that we are nothing and can do nothing without him. In him, we are blessed with every spiritual blessing. The more we embrace our status in Christ as sons and daughters of the Almighty, the more likely we are to step out and accept his call to service because we know that success from God's perspective far outweighs anything that the world might see as failure. Our limitations are vast; however, the God we belong to is limitless. There is nothing he cannot do; nothing is too extraordinary for God, and he desires to reveal that truth through those who trust him.

To become godly leaders who feed Jesus' sheep with excitement, **we must believe nothing is too wonderful for God**. *We must repent of pride—telling God what to do and how to do it, and trust God to do the impossible. As we step into the impossible with God, our understanding of, and faith in, God will grow exponentially.*

Questions for Discussion

1. What seemingly impossible thing(s) has God invited you to participate in?

2. What is your typical first reaction when God calls you to serve?

3. Has fear of failure prevented you from accepting God's call to serve?

4. In what ways do you challenge God's authority?

5. In what way are you intentionally tuning your ear to hear the Shepherd's voice?

6. What obstacles consistently cause you to stumble? What ignorance is God revealing to you?

7. In what areas do you most struggle with humility?

8. Which do you fear more: failure before men or disobedience before God?

9. When have you experienced God miraculously providing for your service or leadership needs?

10. Describe a time when you experienced the glory of God in your leadership.

11. What seemingly impossible call(s) have you chosen to forego? Why?

Chapter 6

What God Requires, God Provides

*For it is God who works in you, both
to will and to work for his good pleasure.
Philippians 2:13*

We want to serve. We want to serve in God's way and for his glory. But what if we don't have what we believe we need to serve, including time, talents, resources, or even faith? Feeling deficient can be one of the most challenging obstacles for a new or seasoned servant who wonders: What if there isn't enough? Will God provide? What if he doesn't? Should we start if we aren't sure we have what we will need to finish?

Perhaps the question of whether we have what we need lies not in God's provision but in our willingness to give back all he has already given us. There is a purpose for everything God has given us; our responsibility is to be aware of what we have received and offer it back to God. We see this perfectly on that hillside with Jesus and the Twelve. *They said to him, "We have only five loaves here and two fish"* (Matthew 14:17).

How would that be enough? It wasn't enough. It was nothing. Perhaps it was worse than nothing, because if it were nothing, no one would eat, and everyone would be in the same hungry boat. What should they, *could* they, do with that little bit? Who would decide what to do with it? Jesus told the Twelve to see what they had, and when they reported back, he told them to bring what they had to him. It's a very meager offering. A pitiful handful. Yet, this very little lunch was precisely what Jesus would use to feed thousands. Jesus was training the Twelve, and us, to trust that God, in his sovereign power, will provide exactly what is needed to fulfill his purpose. God is always in control.

We know the outcome of this miracle: Jesus fed thousands with that little boy's pocket-sized lunch. However, as we unpack this miracle, we discover a feast of lessons. We can identify with the little boy; he brought enough food for himself. Can we identify with his generosity? Are we willing to surrender control over what we have (what we think we need) and give it to Jesus without knowing what he's going to do with it? Maybe. Maybe not.

This wasn't the first time in Scripture that God provided all that was required. When we read about God giving Moses the directions for building the Tabernacle in the desert, we wonder where the Israelites were supposed to get all the building materials: the gold, bronze, and silver, the precious gemstones, the animal hides, and the animals for sacrifices.

In my Sunday School Bible story imagination, I see the Israelites as a rag-tag group of poor, enslaved people who left Egypt with little more than the shirts on their backs, the shoes on their feet, and their bread bowls on their shoulders, narrowly escaping the murderous clutches of Pharaoh! While that may align with Cecil B. DeMille's version, in reality, the Israelites left Egypt with everything they needed—because God ensured that everything was provided. Moses wrote, *The Lord said to Moses, "Yet one plague more I will bring upon Pharaoh and upon Egypt. Afterward he will let you go from here. When he lets you go, he will drive you away completely. Speak now in the hearing of the people, that they ask, every man of his neighbor and every woman of her neighbor, for silver and gold jewelry"... And the Lord had given the people favor in the sight of the Egyptians, so that they let them have what they asked. Thus they plundered the Egyptians* (Exodus 11:1-2; 12:36).

If God has called us to a service or leadership position, perhaps the first step is to examine how much he has already given us—how rich we are. We will be more willing to use what we have when we understand all we have been blessed with. To understand accurately the abundance of what we have received, we need to personally inspect our resources: spiritual, experiential, educational, material, and, of course, the sanctifying presence of the Holy Spirit.

God Provides Spiritual Resources

Let's begin with our spiritual resources in Christ Jesus. God *has blessed us in Christ with every spiritual blessing in the heavenly places* (Ephesians 1:3). As Christians, born again and adopted into the family of God, we know God intimately as our Father, provider, and sustainer. We are blessed beyond measure and can trust him to fulfill every promise he has made to us, blessings that enhance our lives now and eternally. It is simply amazing that, not only do we know God, but he knows us as his children. *See what kind of love the Father has given to us, that we should be called children of God; and so we are* (1 John 3:1). We belong to the family of God, and he lavishes his love upon us; we are wealthy beyond our comprehension. We are *a chosen race, a royal priesthood, a holy nation, a people for his own possession* (1 Peter 2:9).

Our eternal spiritual position, or status, is no longer "in sin." We are now "in Christ," sharing in his glory! We have unlimited and unblocked access to God's throne, where we receive his mercy and grace. Because we have received forgiveness, love, cleansing, unity with God, reconciliation, regeneration, and eternal salvation, we can forgive the offender, love the unlovely, root out bitterness, live holy lives, and be ambassadors of reconciliation. We are empowered to participate in the family business.

We lack nothing because we have received every spiritual blessing in Christ Jesus. We have access to everything we need to prevail. The question is: Do we know how to utilize what we have? Because God has provided for our abundant lives, should we not bring those lives to him so he might use them? What could we possibly lose by surrendering control? Oh, wait, we'd lose control. That's a tall order: to give up control. Most of us love, or even thrive on, being in control. Some dread being out of control, wanting to know where everything is, what is missing, how it can be replaced, what everyone is doing or not doing, and how we can get things done with or without them. Many leaders like control—I'm one of them. I confess that I struggle with this issue. I think that is why God has often placed me in leadership roles where I must rely on him, so I recognize how very little power to regulate I have, and I learn to trust his dominion. In reality, the only thing I can control is how I react to all those things I do not control.

When we struggle with control issues, we tend to hold back what we think we might need later. We might even be considered hoarders. I've seen those houses on TV; you probably have, too: Homes with narrow paths for walking from room to room; things precariously piled from floor to ceiling because people can't give or throw things away. There's an emotional attachment to every item, and the owner is afraid that one day, they'll need it and won't have it. Yikes! Is that what my spirit looks like? Have I hoarded spiritual things because I'm afraid to give them to God for his use? Fearing what will happen if I need them later?

Is that part of why we might dread being asked to serve or step into a leadership position? Are we withholding that which God has given us because we're afraid that if we use it, spend it, or share it, one day we will need it, and it won't be there? Do we hoard because we fear God cannot provide what we'll need now, let alone later?

Sometimes, when we don't want to use what we have, we pray for God to provide other things. We might even ask for something we've already received, for example, forgiveness. As God's children, we have received forgiveness from him, yet we withhold, even hoard, forgiveness, and then we dare to pray and ask God to give us the ability to forgive others. What? We should lavish forgiveness on others; we won't run out; there is no limit to forgiveness. Do we withhold because we want to control who we forgive, and perhaps consider that we can dominate people by withholding our forgiveness from them?

Another spiritual blessing we have received is love; God lavishes his love upon us. Yet, we withhold love. It's not as if there isn't enough love to go around. God is love, and he is the source of love. Maybe we want the power to decide who is lovable and who is not. Do we withhold the riches God has given us? Is this how children of the King are supposed to act? Should we be so stingy when our Father is so abundant?

The King of the universe has adopted us, and every blessing and privilege of the firstborn is ours. God bestows grace upon each one of his children, and he doesn't hold back. He saturates our lives with every good and perfect gift, and his mercies are new every morning. Yet, we fear telling others that this precious blessing is available for them. Are we afraid that God won't have sufficient grace or mercy, and we might miss out? What do we fear? That we won't speak with the right words? That we'll say the wrong thing at the wrong time? That we can't control the moment or the outcome? The ambiguity often terrifies and paralyzes us. We shouldn't fear whether we share correctly; we just need to share. If we don't, we are holding on too tightly to what we've received.

One way we give back to God the spiritual blessings he has given us is to testify to others about what he is doing in our lives. As we see his hand of grace upholding us, sense his power enabling us, experience his

Word directing us, and receive answers to one prayer after another, we must tell others how God is changing, guiding, and undergirding us. We must return God's blessings to him in worshipful praise. We are to praise him personally and in the company of other people. As we give back to God by proclaiming what he is doing in our lives, he becomes more famous and then multiplies and uses the praise and glory we offer for his good purposes. More people will come to Jesus as we give back our spiritual blessings in praise, honor, and recognition of who God is and what he is doing. More people will be built up, comforted, and encouraged. When others hear how God is blessing you and me, they will want to be a part of God's family, too, drawn by the blessings of God's goodness, power, and love. Isn't that the essence of service, to lead others to Jesus?

God has given us a wealth of spiritual blessings; we give them back in praise, trusting God to use whatever we give to benefit others. We cannot deplete our spiritual blessings; the more we forgive, the more readily we will be to forgive. The more we love, the more our capacity for love increases. The more we speak about God, the easier it becomes to share Truth with others. The more we step out and trust God with every outcome, the more he is glorified. We don't need to fear using the spiritual blessings we've been given. We know through continual affirmation that God is in control of everything, and we will always have what we need.

The only reason we might not have enough to feed others is if we allow our blessing flow to dry up. When was the last time you saw God at work in your life? When was the last time you had an answered prayer? When was the last time you walked in his power? If your last encounter with God was so long ago that you don't recall it, perhaps you have not recently relinquished control long enough to come to God's table and partake of all he can provide. If you are starving spiritually, ask yourself: How long has it been since I had a spiritual feast with God? How long ago did I take time to eat of the Bread of Life and drink of the Living Water? Have I been so busy trying to maintain control, seeing that everyone else is fed, that I have failed to receive what God has for me? Take time regularly to belly up to God's table, fill your plate with his promises, drink deep of the joy of salvation, and count your blessings, becoming aware of how much you have to offer back for his good purposes. You have been gifted with spiritual resources; tap into them.

God Provides Experiential Resources

In addition to our spiritual blessings, we have also received or collected life experiences. Not all our life experiences as Christians are positive; some are very good, others are not. We enjoy dwelling on the good, and we often may want to forget the bad. But everything we go through in life becomes a part of who we are. And God uses each of our life experiences as we offer them back to him.

It is easy to think that God will use our good times and memories, but it is often difficult to believe he could—or would—use the bad. Nevertheless, why would God allow us either suffering or rejoicing if he did not intend to use every moment in some way—for the good of others, our eternal good, or his eternal glory? What would be the purpose of any life experience if we were not to offer it up to God so that he might use it in some way, large or small, for his excellent purpose?

Yes, there are some experiences we would just as soon forget; I'm sure King David had one or two that he'd prefer not to remember, but of course, many of his missteps have been recorded for all time. Nevertheless, as we read about David's life, times of failure, heartache, suffering, and yes, even great rejoicing, we are touched in consequential ways and in places nothing else could reach. We identify with biblical characters through their experiences, and our faith grows as we learn more about God through how he ministers to his people. Reading about how God dealt with people who lived thousands of years ago and seeing the same loving discipline and guiding hand at work in our lives enables us to develop the traits we need to serve other needy people.

Personally, there are people in the Bible that I intimately identify with, people who have endured heartache and shame. Being reminded that these sinful and sinned against people were still loved by God and welcomed into his family is a life-changing reassurance for me. As a person who endured sexual abuse as a child, my understanding of love, worth, and acceptance was tainted by that sin and its consequences. I made irresponsible decisions based on my flawed thinking and, for years, lived with the shame of the life experiences thrust upon me. I was married to my husband for nineteen years before I could tell him my shameful secret of sexual abuse. Nineteen years.

I can attest that when we give our sufferings back to God, he will use them mightily. God has given me a platform to encourage others by sharing that, although the world has tried to heap the same shame on them, they don't have to carry it. Even when our grief comes from our own sin, we can release it—because Jesus died on the cross to make us whole. Our history does not determine our worth. His story determines our worth! We are worth more than the choicest jewels; we are worth the blood of Jesus. For many years, I chose to try to control my life by holding on to my secret and pain, believing the lie that I should feel shame, but that helped no one, especially not me. However, when I gave my pain over to Jesus, like the little boy who let go of his lunch and his control over that lunch, Jesus used my offering to minister to many people.

The Twelve had to learn to follow a child's lead; they had to learn to release their control of the situation, which they didn't have anyway, and bring what they had to Jesus. What can you bring to Jesus? Abuse, divorce, infidelity, addiction, death, depression, abortion? Whatever your suffering and whatever your shame, Jesus will use it. The depth of pain you endured doesn't match the depth of forgiveness and restoration waiting for you. Your experiences are touchpoints of commonality with other suffering souls. As we share our life experiences, God uses them to allow us to come alongside a brother or sister and help them bear their burden; we are more compassionate and effective as leaders when we know by experience how heavy the burden is.

Our spiritual and experiential resources often seem meager to us because we don't have the perspective God has. We see through the same moral and finite lens that the Twelve used. We can only see what we can see with our eyes and no more, but God sees and knows everything. God sees the hurting, hopeless, confused, and searching soul. He knows what is needed to feed the lost sheep and provides the resources to meet that need. Someone came alongside each of us, sharing their life and the gospel with us; should we not be as willing as they were? Whatever sufferings God has used to grow our faith and produce spiritual maturity in us are resources God has given us so that we might help someone else. Therefore, we should bring everything to God so that he might use it for his good purpose. Your experiential resources are valuable; utilize them.

God Provides Educational Resources

Not only does God bestow spiritual blessings upon us and give us a life full of experiences, but he also provides educational resources. He has given us the ability to read, write, and communicate with people. We are intelligent. And many of us live in a culture that embraces education; most of us attended elementary and high school, and many have gone beyond that. Some of us have more letters after our names than in our names.

It is common for an individual to have the opportunity to attend church weekly and be taught God's Holy Word. Bible studies are readily available—from online classes to in-home small groups. We can listen to the Word of God on our phones and set up daily verses for our inboxes. For most people, there is no excuse for not being educated in God's Word, as God has given us the intelligence to learn how to read His Word. However, the most essential educational guide to our spiritual education is the Holy Spirit. Despite what opportunities we are afforded, there is no replacement for the Spirit's wisdom and guidance poured into us continually. God wants to connect with us through His Word, and He goes to great lengths to do so.

Not only do we need to read God's Word, but we must also apply it. We must do what it says, which is how we are sanctified. Sanctification is the process through which the Holy Spirit matures us. As we avail ourselves of the Words of God and the inner workings of the Holy Spirit, we grow in grace and wisdom. We apply what we've learned. And when we do, our lives become different from those around us who are not in Christ. Our education, as God's children, changes us. We were created to stand out and be different; therefore, hiding or blending in is nearly impossible. You have been called to be a leader for a reason: you look like one.

We must not simply read God's Words; we must let his Words read us. The Bible reveals much about God, but it also shows us much about ourselves, and as we read and apply it, we become more and more equipped to live worthy of the gospel, to live lives of submission. Our biblical education does not puff us up with useless knowledge; it teaches us how to love God and others. We show our love for God by submitting to him. When we offer ourselves to God, he uses our service for his glory. As we apply what we've learned, we live more beautifully, gently, lovingly, and graciously different from the world.

But do we sincerely want to be different from everyone else? Maybe not. Maybe this is precisely why we don't utilize our education as a tool or resource God has given us to advance his kingdom. Perhaps we're afraid others will react or respond to our differences negatively. But isn't being different exactly what Moses asked of God before he left Sinai with the Israelites?

"If your presence will not go with me, do not bring us up from here. For how shall it be known that I have found favor in your sight, I and your people? Is it not in your going with us, so that we are distinct, I and your people, from every other people on the face of the earth?" (Exodus 33:15-17).

As we resist conformity to the culture, deviate from its determined norms, and swim against its current, we offer ourselves to God to be used for his good purpose. We say to God, "Yes, your way is best. It is safest. It is wisest. It is healthiest." Our lives become praise offerings and worship to God. We proclaim God's way to a lost world by living differently, peaceably, non-judgmentally, and non-threateningly. However, we cannot control how the world will receive that message. We will probably be hated and persecuted and have to endure suffering. The world won't understand us. And, rather than thinking we are well-educated, it will insist that we are ignorant and intolerant. But Jesus says that's OK; the world hated him first. If his presence is with us, if we have learned to contend for the gospel without being contentious, then any suffering is a badge of honor. You have educational resources; apply them.

God Provides Material Resources

We have material resources: houses, cars, clothes, food, and money. Some of us have much. Some of us barely get by. In every case, everything we have is a gift from God; even the *power to get wealth* (Deuteronomy 8:18) is from God. However much or little we have, we must still ask: How much do we offer back to God? Material resources, especially money, are probably the hardest things to release control over because it is so clearly necessary for survival in the world. We know that money is not evil; it is the *love of money [that] is a root of all kinds of evils* (1 Timothy 6:10). We also know we cannot serve two masters. Jesus told us, *"No one can serve two masters, for either he will hate the one and love the other, or he will be devoted to the one and despise the other. You cannot serve God and money"* (Matthew 6:24).

It is easy to hold money in higher esteem than we should. We tend to equate money with control, and we fear losing control over our financial lives. What if we cannot buy food, pay the rent, or plan for retirement? Why is it so hard to trust God with our finances? Why is it so hard to trust God with the finances of the organizations or churches in which we serve? Perhaps it is because we fear that God's standards for our lives and ministries are not quite the same as our standards. We don't want less than we currently have, and we are afraid that God's bar for a comfortable life or a powerful ministry might not be as high as we'd like it to be. Yet, the testimonies of people who boldly trust in God's provision convict us.

There was a time when the child of one of the teen moms I mentored needed glasses. My young mom, a new believer, didn't have the money because she had written a tithe check that week. But let's face it, there is never enough money when you are a 20-year-old single mom of a 4-year-old. Yet, this struggling young mom who joyfully wrote her tithe check a few days before, now needed that money.

I wanted to take control, swoop in, rescue her, and write a check for the glasses. Before I could grab my checkbook, God put it on my heart to hold back. (Well, that and the fact that we were involved in a Christian program that strongly discouraged us from being the girls' rescuers. Why? Because our rescuing them prevented God from rescuing them.) And then, before

I could speak, this young woman quietly stated, "I know God will take care of us; he always does." So, I prayed with her; I prayed that God would honor her faith and his name. God tells us to test him in this, to bring our tithes and see if he will not throw open the floodgates of heaven and pour out so much blessing that there will not be room enough to store it (Malachi 3:10).

The next day, when this precious new believer went to get her mail, there was a check from the state. Her baby's father had a new job, and the court-ordered support was precisely the cost of the glasses. I'm still praising God for this young mother's faith and how he provided for her. She is still praising God. And now, years later, she has a big job in a laboratory at a large company. Not only does she continue to tithe, but she is also giving her time and finances to the same ministry that helped support her. When we give back to God through the finances he has given us, he blesses the gift and uses it in ways we cannot imagine. Because God promises to meet our needs, why should we fear withholding anything from him? You have material blessings; don't be afraid to use them.

God Provides the Holy Spirit

Before Jesus returned to heaven, he promised the disciples that he would *"ask the Father, and he will give you another Helper, to be with you forever, even the Spirit of truth, whom the world cannot receive, because it neither sees him nor knows him. You know him, for he dwells with you and will be in you"* (John 14:16-17). When God saves us, He justifies us and gives us the Holy Spirit.

Being justified means that God declares that we are in right standing before him based on Jesus' achievement. But that doesn't mean there isn't work for God to do in us to make us holy. The sacrifice of Jesus made us right with God, but God is still at work in us. *For by a single offering he has perfected for all times those who are being sanctified* (Hebrews 10:14). We have far to go to be made holy. When we were saved, God reckoned Christ's righteousness to us; therefore, we stand (our status before God) in Jesus' perfection. But that isn't all; our imperfection was reckoned onto Christ (he was made sin for us). We still have weaknesses that must be worked out, but we have the Holy Spirit dwelling inside of us to accomplish this work. Sanctification is the ongoing work of the Holy Spirit in our lives. God changes us as we cooperate with his Spirit by availing ourselves of prayer, studying the Word of God, fellowshipping with other believers, and serving God's people. He changes our character, actions, attitudes, and thought patterns. This process of sanctification means we are being made holy; holiness is our destiny; it is what God is doing in us through his Holy Spirit. Obedience allows us to see God, and his presence transforms us.

Who we are today is most likely not who we will be next week or next year because God is busy making us into the image of Christ Jesus and promises that he will complete the work that he has begun. Yet, who we are right now is exactly who God intends to use for his good purpose today. We don't have to wait until we are entirely sanctified and spiritually mature to be of use to God; God will use our service to sanctify and mature us. God is about the business of making us holy!

We must not think that we are required to wait until we become our version of perfection before surrendering control of our lives and offering them to God for his use. If God calls us to service, he has given or will provide all we need to serve; we only need to lay before him what we have and who we are now. What we may perceive as a weakness could be the strength God intends to use for his good purpose. What we have and who we are right now is sufficient.

Ironically, the things we perceive as weaknesses or places of shame often become the arenas in which we are most trained to battle against the forces of darkness. When we surrender control in these places to Jesus and follow his instructions, his presence is revealed, souls are healed, and we become powerful agents for advancing the kingdom.

God knew exactly what was available to the Twelve as they stood on that hillside with all those hungry people. Jesus did not tell them to go and see what was available because he wondered what they would find; he sent them so *they could see* what he had already provided. Jesus knew they would balk at having so little. He knew them well, and he knows us just as well. He knows our strengths and weaknesses. He knows who we were, who we are, and who we are becoming.

We may feel insufficient because we don't have an alphabet behind our names, we are young, we are new to the Christian faith, or simply because we've never held a position of service before. Or, we may feel insufficient because we've burned out, feel used up, or tired—having given until we've nothing left to give. Let me assure you that if you are serving through the power of the Holy Spirit within you, he will supply you with the power you need to complete that which he has called you to. If you are not serving with his power, you will surely run dry. Jesus fed a multitude through the lunch of one little boy who was surrendered to Jesus. And right now, God has given you precisely what you need to provide for the ones he's given you. We don't know *how* God will use us, but we know he will, if we are surrendered to him. We can't control how he will choose to use us, but we can control whether or not we offer ourselves for his use. Whatever God has given us, let us bring it to him without an agenda and watch what he does. You have the Holy Spirit within you; let him flow through you.

When We Are Faithful with a Little, More Is Given

We have spiritual blessings, life experiences, educational and material resources, the Holy Spirit, and our lives. Every day we wake up able to breathe air is a gift of life from God. Granted, for some of us, as we grow older, getting out of bed can be the most difficult part of the day. For those fighting depression or illness, life can be emotionally, physically, and spiritually challenging. Everyone has burdens, but life continues, and as long as we are breathing, God has work for us to do. We may not like the hand we've been dealt, but our responsibility is to play it in a way that honors God because God has seen fit to let us live another day. As long as there is breath in our lungs and blood coursing through our veins, shouldn't we give that life as an offering to God, fully surrendered, so that he might use it for his glory?

To think that we have nothing worth bringing to God that he can multiply for his purpose and plans means that we have stopped trusting God to be God and have limited him to acting within what we can control. When we try to remain in control, we insist that God work within our boundaries and the limitations of our humanness, and we minimize God's greatness and expose our lack of faith. We arrogantly treat God as an exalted version of ourselves by limiting him to our human perspective and understanding. We fail to tap into the glorious wisdom of God when we rely on our pitiful worldly wisdom. That's when we decide our problems are no longer solvable.

In our desperation to rely entirely on what we think we can control, see, grasp, or understand, we often fail to live humbly before God in faith. Instead, we live in the pride of our abilities, and that is choosing to live in worldly wisdom. Worldly wisdom is unspiritual and produces bitter jealousy and selfish ambition (James 3:13-18). As we struggle to solve every problem independently of God, seeking our resources first or scheming to come up with a solution, we live in self-focused arrogance. Of course, we would probably call it something other than that; we'd say we are self-sufficient, resourceful, or capable. Until we aren't.

When we anchor our trust and confidence in our abilities and ourselves, we fall into a two-fold trap that we probably don't recognize: We harbor selfish ambitions while we envy others who seem more accomplished than we are. This is not living humbly; this is not living in godly wisdom. In earthly wisdom, we rely on ourselves and do not fear God, but fear failure. *This is not the wisdom that comes down from above, but is earthly, unspiritual, demonic* (James 3:15). Demonic—God's words, not mine.

Living by worldly wisdom invites us to compare ourselves to other people, including their service, successes, and yes, perhaps even their failures. We endlessly peruse others' social media posts, book sales, ministry events, church buildings, and websites; we envy their followers, likes, friends, bookings, parishioners, and publications. Envy and selfish ambition distort our vision; all we can see is what we are missing, and that's when we feel insufficient and unimportant. When we focus on other people and what they have or are doing, it is easy to forget that we've been given precisely everything we need to do all that God would have us do.

When we compare ourselves to others, we will always assume that we are lacking. We may believe we have nothing of value to bring to the table—less than a few loaves of bread and a couple of fish, or that we *are* nothing, and therefore, we are useless. Comparison always breeds discontent, discontent breeds grumbling, and grumbling breeds failure. This wisdom is not pure, peace-loving, considerate, submissive, full of mercy and good fruit, impartial, or sincere. It is not of God.

Such earthly wisdom is impure because it doubts the sovereignty and majesty of God. It limits God to only what we can control, see, and understand. It is not peace-loving—creating chaos in the soul, disturbing our rest in the sufficiency of God. It is not considerate—not allowing for grace toward others or ourselves. It is not submissive—dictating to God what he, or we, can or cannot do based on whatever fear or paradigm of failure we use. Earthly wisdom has no mercy, kindness, or leniency. Instead, it feeds our lack of confidence and brutally tears and thrashes in rebellion against our desire to live contentedly where God has placed us. It produces no fruit because it fails to serve. It is not impartial—preventing us from honestly evaluating ourselves or accurately perceiving and embracing the grace God has given us.

Godly wisdom is wisdom that comes from God as we ask for it. We should ask because the Bible instructs us to: *If any of you lacks wisdom, let him ask God, who gives generously to all without reproach* (James 1:5). As we seek God's wisdom, we abandon independence and control, wholly leaning on the power of Almighty God to accomplish whatever task he has given us with whatever resources he has provided. Godly wisdom rests peacefully in the knowledge of God's ultimate perfection in the timing and provision of his gifts. It is an unobstructed conduit of grace and forgiveness to others and allows us to accept what God has given and trust that whatever he has withheld is for our good. Godly wisdom extends mercy and kindness; it listens, trusts, and seeks to help. It enables us to understand that there is contentment and peace in surrendering to God and trusting in him.

Godly wisdom thrives in contentment rather than comparison. When we live in contentment, we live with an openness to receive whatever the Lord would give us, are grateful for what we have received, and are generous to give back to him everything we have. We are wise enough to understand that whatever we have is not ours to hold onto anyway. We also know that whatever we have is sufficient for us at this moment because in the next moment, we may have less, or we may have more. In addition, we grasp that whatever anyone else has or doesn't have is precisely what God has given to or withheld from them for his good purposes. There is no room for comparison in godly wisdom.

God is all-wise; he knows what we need and is able to accomplish what he has planned for us. God's wisdom does not consist of just the knowledge of all things; it includes the perfect comprehension of the most beneficial goals and the strategic timing and precisely flawless means to accomplish those goals. God alone is all-wise; his ways are much higher than ours, and his thoughts are much higher. We must not limit God to only what we can manage or imagine.

While we may think that we know what God is doing or planning, the reality is that he's orchestrating a multitude of strategies around us, through us, and deep within us that we are ignorant of and may not even be fully cognizant of when the work is complete. We must recognize that he is using our circumstances to accomplish his goals in our lives, and we can trust that we will remain in these circumstances as long as necessary for him to complete his purpose in them. We must beware of looking at our resources with skepticism or bitterness. Because what we have and what we don't have is precisely what God has provided and is using. *"Who has known the mind of the Lord, or who has been his counselor? Or who has given a gift to him, that he might be repaid?" For from him and through him and to him are all things. To him be glory forever* (Romans 11:33-36).

As we trust God's wisdom, we can know that he has provided and withheld expertly; he has given us precisely what we need to serve and glorify him.

We know what happened next in this event in the life of the Twelve: Jesus miraculously multiplied the pitiful offering, feeding thousands. A miracle is something only God can do. Look at what God has given you. Is there anything you have that God has not given to you? No. Look at the miracles God has worked in your life thus far: You are a new creation, living in Christ Jesus. You are no longer living in the kingdom of darkness but are alive in the kingdom of light. And you have a power within you that can accomplish more than you can ask or imagine.

God has given you much, and what God has given, he requires. God gives us all that we need to serve where and how he calls us. Our responsibility is to be faithful with what he has given; only then will he give more. Only he knows what that "more" will look like. We must surrender control of that as well. As we submit to him and use all that he gives us, we will be amazed at how many people are fed, and we will be surprised at the person he is making us into.

We must be faithful where he has placed us and serve the ones he has put before us. We cannot multiply ourselves or our gifts and blessings on our own. We need God to do that. He does it as we surrender control and trust him to provide everything we need. We must not be afraid to bring him all he asks of us. We must not be afraid that we won't have enough of whatever we need to finish the work. Starting with much does not guarantee a good ending. Starting and continuing with God ensures success, and God is the definer of what that success will look like.

The Twelve brought the little boy's lunch. They did not know what Jesus was going to do. We may think we know what he will do with us, through us, and for us, but perhaps he plans something more miraculous than we could ever hope or imagine. What you have right now is enough. Will you bring all that you have and trust God to do with it what he will?

To become godly leaders who feed Jesus' sheep in complete trust, we must **believe that whatever God requires of us, he has already provided for us.** *We must repent of the desire to be in control and to hoard our gifts. We will overcome the fears that prevent us from taking on God's work as we surrender all that he has provided back to him.*

Questions for Discussion

1. List the spiritual blessings/resources you have received from God.

2. Write out the experiential blessings/resources you have received.

3. Identify your material blessings/resources.

4. What educational blessings/resources has God given you?

5. What blessings/resources are you surrendering control of and bringing to God for his use and glory? What blessings/resources are you withholding from God? Why?

6. What intentional disciplines are you practicing to work with God in your sanctification?

7. Does the way you compare yourself unfavorably to others distract you from serving God's people?

8. In what areas do you struggle most with relinquishing control?

Chapter 7

There Is No Confusion in God

For God is not a God of confusion but of peace.
But all things should be done decently and in order.
1 Corinthians 14:33a, 40

Are you sure this is what God would have you do? Doubt and confusion can make us feel that it is impossible to know the will of God for our ministry or service, and when we aren't sure, we often don't move forward. It's easy to let the disorder of our lives, the chaos of the world, or our limited knowledge of God paralyze us. What if there is only one correct path? We surely don't want to step off of it or inadvertently onto the wrong path. But what if there isn't only one path? What if there are several good options? How do we choose? God does not leave us guessing, nor does he lead us into confusion. God is a God of order; he directed the Twelve with clarity and order, and he will similarly guide us.

It was a beautiful spring day, and all of the circumstances were perfectly aligned for the miracle that we now know was about to happen; but no hungry person on that hillside had any idea what Jesus was about to do. The Twelve did not know—they only saw that they had a little bit of food and there were a whole lot of hungry people. This was indeed a moment that required order and organization. Jesus took control and ordered the Twelve, who then organized the crowd. There were no options other than to follow Jesus; everyone knew enough to do whatever he told them. *And he said to his disciples, "Have them sit down in groups of about fifty each."*

And they did so, and had them all sit down (Luke 9:14b–15) *Now there was much grass in the place. So the men sat down, about five thousand in number* (John 6:10b).

Jesus' instructions perfectly aligned with every detail of the circumstances of this situation. He told the disciples to have the people sit down, which was perfectly acceptable as the weather was nice, the grass was green, and there was plenty of room. We assume peace and order prevailed as the Twelve obeyed and the people sat. Everyone acted squarely in the clear, distinct will of God. There was no confusion, chaos, or questioning.

It was easy for the Twelve and the multitude to know God's will for the evening because Jesus directed them. Have you ever wished, prayed, and hoped that you were acting in the orderly will of God, but you just weren't sure? Have you found yourself wishing Jesus would direct you more distinctly to do this or do that? I know I have. We desire to stay within the will of God for our lives, but how do we know for sure we can or that we are? Can we know?

Do you wish God would speak to you, telling you what to do and how to lead the same way he addressed the Twelve that afternoon—in a clear, audible voice? Have you ever been paralyzed, unable to decide on, begin, or continue a task, because you were afraid that you might act outside of the will of God, or worse yet, lead others to step outside of his will? Fear of bringing dishonor to his name through disobedience or misunderstanding can stop us before we begin, causing us to forfeit the ability to serve God's people. How much do we lose because we unnecessarily question our ability to hear (and then follow) God's orderly instructions?

As we look at the way Jesus taught the Twelve and trained them in godly leadership skills, we will learn that we can know the will of God for our place of service because God is a God of order, and he works in an orderly fashion. As we overcome the disorder in our lives and thoughts by walking with God and embracing his orderliness, we can serve his people without fear of being disobedient. We can know the will of God and confidently act on it.

God doesn't leave us in the dark, guessing what we need to do to accomplish his goals; he provides us with a roadmap to know his will. Ultimately, his will for us is to understand and obey his written Word. He will never ask us to do anything that contradicts Scripture. When God calls us to serve and to lead his people, he gives us the means to confirm the call by asking: Does it align with his Word? Does it align with my circumstances? Do I have peace in obedience? The alignment of his Word, our circumstances, and our inner peace is the anchor we need to know that we are firmly in God's plans. Did these three align for the Twelve? Let's see.

Alignment with the Word of God: Jesus' instructions to the Twelve perfectly aligned with God's character and written Word. The first step in understanding God's will is asking: Is there harmony between what we believe is being asked of us and the Word of God? We need a deep understanding of God's Word to recognize this alignment, which the Holy Spirit will give us when we seek it. *And so, from the day we heard, we have not ceased to pray for you, asking that you may be filled with the knowledge of his will in all spiritual wisdom and understanding, so as to walk in a manner worthy of the Lord, fully pleasing to him: bearing fruit in every good work and increasing in the knowledge of God* (Colossians 1:9-10).

Jesus' commands will never fall out of alignment with the written Word. He told the Twelve to feed the people; we see examples of God feeding his people from the beginning. Adam and Eve had a bountiful garden from which to eat, the Israelites had manna in the desert for forty years, and on and on.

After Jesus called the Twelve to serve, he told them what to do and how to do it orderly. Throughout Scripture, we see God's order. They probably had questions because there was no food, but like the Twelve, we must begin wherever Jesus tells us.

Alignment with our circumstances: The second criterion for discerning God's will for us is whether what God tells us to do aligns with our circumstances. We see that what Jesus told them to do on that hillside fully aligned with the circumstances around them. God works in and through our circumstances, not apart from them. *And we know that for those who love God all things work together for good, for those who are called according to his purpose* (Romans 8:28).

Jesus told the Twelve to have the people sit, and there was room to sit. It was spring, with plenty of green grass to accommodate every man, woman, and child. The people clearly understood the instructions, and they sat. They didn't have to cut down trees to make more room or ask some to leave because there wasn't sufficient room.

Alignment with peace in obedience: Thirdly, we know we are in God's will when peace prevails, and here, we see that peace prevailed: there was order and organization. *And let the peace of Christ rule in your hearts, to which indeed you were called in one body. And be thankful* (Colossians 3:15).

Everyone on that hillside was tuned in to Jesus, and peace prevailed. Peace does not mean the absence of fear or anxiety or that every detail is figured out and every loose end is tied. Some people may have been complaining about their space on the hillside—peace does not mean the absence of questions. Peace also doesn't mean everything is comfortably known; the people still didn't have sufficient food, nor did they know where it would come from, if at all. Peace is an inner, quiet understanding that God is in control; it is obedience, no matter what we don't know.

It's one thing to look back and see the Twelve empowered to serve with confidence and understanding because they had the alignment of God's

Word, their circumstances, and inner peace, but what about us? In the busyness of our lives, how do we discern God's will for us as leaders? How can we know if what we believe God is asking us to do aligns with his Word? How can we know if our circumstances align? How can we know if we have inner peace or are just not seeing all the hurdles? How can we know for sure that all three components are in harmony?

First, we need to recognize our weaknesses and selfish desires. We know it is possible to manipulate God's Word to say what we want, to engineer circumstances to fit our desires, and there's no denying that we can mistake the absence of fear for peace. But it is nigh impossible to simultaneously bring all three components into harmony without rigging something. Therefore, absent our selfish superintending, when these three align, because God is a God of order, it seems more than plausible that the plans we are pondering are, in fact, within the will of God.

God wants us to understand his will. He tells us that when we offer ourselves fully to him (surrendering our rights to ourselves) and refrain from indulging in the culture's pattern, instead choosing to renew our minds as we study his Word, we can test and approve what his good, pleasing, and perfect will is for us. As we saturate ourselves in his Word, we can better understand the character of God and recognize that he will never ask us or command us to do anything contrary to his character. Because his will is *good, acceptable, and perfect* (Romans 12:2), whatever God asks us to do will always be good, acceptable, and perfect.

God is eternal, and his character is eternally unchanging. *And also the Glory of Israel will not lie or have regret, for he is not a man, that he should have regret* (1 Samuel 15:29). There has never been a time when God wasn't exactly as he is now—and there never will be. God does not transform or morph into more of himself; he is always fully God. We cannot add to God or take away from God. Therefore, because God is eternal and unchanging, we know that God's wisdom has always been complete; there is nothing for God to learn, and there is no new set of facts that would mean he would have to change his mind or make a new plan. You and I, unlike God, continually learn and change our minds and plans to incorporate additional knowledge. God already knows everything. Everything that ever was, is, or will be.

God is not fickle; he does not act arbitrarily. All of his actions and decisions are made with the full knowledge of all that has ever been, is now, or ever will be. God does not wait for our response or reaction and then plot or plan his next move; he already knows what we will do before we do anything, and he already knows what he will do next and next and next. God is a God of order; his thoughts are ordered, his ways are ordered, and his words are ordered. There is no confusion in God. Therefore, let us break down the necessary components that must align for us to know the will of God.

The Power of God's Word

The perfect revelation of God's order is chronicled in the creation account in Genesis. Each day was designed perfectly to support and sustain what would be created each subsequent day. We also see his order in the seasons: spring always follows winter, summer follows spring, autumn follows summer, and winter follows autumn. We see his order in the skies when we study the perfect placement of the sun and the planets in the universe. All creation and its sustenance are accomplished with his Word: God spoke, and everything came into being. *For the word of the Lord is upright, and all his work is done in faithfulness. He loves righteousness and justice; the earth is full of the steadfast love of the Lord. By the word of the Lord the heavens were made, and by the breath of his mouth all their host. He gathers the waters of the sea as a heap; he puts the deeps in storehouses.*

Let all the earth fear the Lord; let all the inhabitants of the world stand in awe of him! For he spoke and it came to be; he commanded, and it stood firm (Psalm 33:4-9).

We cannot separate God's character, Word, and work. His character is true; therefore, his words will always be true, and he will never contradict himself in his actions or call. Yet, how do we know when, or if, he is speaking to us personally? We may hear what we believe is the voice of God leading us to act, but unlike the Twelve, who had Jesus speaking to them face to face, we wonder if we can know for sure. First, we must learn to recognize our Shepherd's voice; the first way we do that is to spend time with him.

We train our ears to hear the Lord's voice as we spend time in his Word, becoming more familiar with the overarching account of God's recorded events throughout history and his sovereign involvement in the lives of people and nations as he brought about his determined purposes and plans. We learn to recognize his voice as we listen to him speaking to the ancients and study his patterns. We master the sound of his voice as he becomes more than a Bible story, and we learn that his voice will be in the likeness of Bible accounts. Our Shepherd's voice will sound a lot like the way the Bible reads.

As we grow accustomed to hearing God through the Scriptures, we must be careful not to take God's words and promises out of context. It is wise to be on guard so that we don't misinterpret parables or appropriate for ourselves something not intended for us. For example, God's call to Abraham to leave his country was a literal but personal command; it is not a calling for us to pack up and move right now. However, if, for example, we believe God may be calling us to a mission field away from home, we can surely use this biblical account as confirmation that when we obediently follow God's call to step out of our comfort zone, God will go with us.

God's call to us will never contradict his Word; his Word will confirm what he would have us do. As he was with Abraham, so will he be with us.

God may speak to us through the godly counsel of other Christians, and when he does, their counsel will always align with God's written words in Scripture. Our pastors, teachers, and friends who spend time in the Word of God may be the very ones through whom that counsel comes. However, we must not rely entirely upon God's use of other people to direct us. Every decision can and should be verified through direct communication with God in prayer and by seeking confirmation in his Word. God will guide us through his written words in the Bible.

God might also speak to us through our desires. God's Word tells us he is the One who *works in you, both to will and to work for his good pleasure* (Philippians 2:13). It is not unlike God to give us the will and desire, and then present us with an opportunity that aligns with that desire. I have heard it said that if we want a specific job or position, we are being selfish, prideful, or ambitious to pursue it. Maybe. Maybe not. I've also heard some people say that if we do not want to do something, we can rest assured that is precisely what God would have us do. Maybe. Maybe not. There may be a hint of truth to both of those thoughts, but I'm not sure either position is reliable as a general rule in most situations.

It seems more plausible that if we desire to serve or lead, and if that desire is in line with God's character and Word, he has most likely worked within us and is now calling us to action. If we have a passion—if God has put the desire in our hearts, and if there is no selfish motivation—then God will equip us to act on that desire as we seek his equipping.

Still, we must be careful not to follow our hearts' desires without confirmation that our desires align with God's Word and character. *The heart is deceitful above all things, and desperately sick; who can understand it?* (Jeremiah 17:9). We've been warned: We cannot figure out our hearts.

Therefore, we must not run hither and yon, racing after every desire we are drawn to. Even as godly servant leaders, we cannot be all things to all people. We must test the spirits (1 John 4:1) to discern whether our desires are from God, and the first test is: Do our desires align with the written words of God?

God also speaks to us through the Holy Spirit. As the Holy Spirit prompts us, and as we obey and act immediately upon those promptings, we effectively tune our ears to hear God's voice. It's like tuning a radio in the old days; as we obey, we sync our ears to the frequency upon which the Spirit of God speaks. He may talk to you differently than he does to your friends or me, but as you earnestly seek him, you will learn his voice.

Just as we have to be intentional to learn God's voice, there are also things we do that prevent us from hearing him. When we think we've heard God, and yet our first inclination is to run to other people for their input or, worse yet, debate with God, we begin to tune him out. We invite static into the conversation. Why would we do that? Maybe it's when we want to avoid hearing what he tells us.

As you commit to learning your Shepherd's voice, Jesus gives you a precious promise: God's people know their Shepherd's voice and will not follow a stranger. He taught, *"When he has brought out all his own, he goes before them, and the sheep follow him, for they know his voice. A stranger they will not follow, but they will flee from him, for they do not know the voice of strangers"* (John 10:4-5).

We have the added security of knowing that our Shepherd's voice will never contradict the written Word of God because Jesus said, *"I and the Father are one"* (John 10:30). Once we hear God speak to us, our responsibility is to obey, as our Lord Jesus Christ did perfectly. We desire to obey God because, like Jesus, we love the Father.

Jesus, our substitute, endured the full force of the wrath of God on the cross when, in obedience to the Father, he became sin on our behalf. He submitted his will to the Father because he knew the character of the Father, the orderliness of God, and that the narrative of the entirety of Scripture pointed to him. He is the Messiah who suffered in our place that we might be saved through him. Jesus learned obedience, not from disobedience (as is the case with us), but through life's experiences, from what he suffered (Hebrews 5:8). He did not need to learn how to obey; he obeyed perfectly every time, in every way, and in that obedience, he was made perfect (complete). He was *made perfect* (Hebrews 5:9), not from imperfection, but through a life of righteousness and obedience. Jesus was the fulfillment, the completion, of the Law of Moses. In his perfection, he was the one and only tool that could accomplish our salvation and provide the righteousness we need to stand before a holy God. God's plan for our service will fully align with God's Word, and our obedience will reflect our love for the Father and the Son.

The Perfection of Our Circumstances

In addition to corresponding with his Word and character, the second criterion for discerning God's will for us is knowing that his plans will align with our circumstances. In other words, we will never need to scheme, plot, or manipulate things to fit God's request into our lives. We can trust that he has already perfectly orchestrated and ordered our circumstances to correlate with the work he has for us.

Nothing is too complicated for God; no circumstance can hinder his plans, and he surely doesn't need our limited wisdom, cunning, or trickery to help him. If we are being called and don't see our circumstances aligning with that call, we must ask God to show us our circumstances as he sees them. When he calls us, we can trust that he has perfectly ordered things so we can fulfill his purpose. If they don't, either we are not seeing them correctly or we are not hearing God clearly. If our situation seems impossible to overcome, then we either aren't operating in faith or we are trying to manipulate our calling. If God has called you, you can trust that he is also working in your circumstances surrounding that call, and God's plans will not be thwarted. *The Lord brings the counsel of the nations to nothing; he frustrates the plans of the people. The counsel of the Lord stands forever, the plans of his heart to all generations* (Psalm 33:10-11).

Nothing can hinder God nor prevent him from accomplishing his plans and purposes for the world and for us. He created the world from nothing, and he opens and closes the wombs. God controls all of nature; he caused an ax head to float and changed water into wine. He healed the blind, the deaf, the lame, and even raised the dead—God can certainly handle or change anything about our situation. Perhaps our seemingly overwhelming circumstances, which God has purposefully ordained or allowed, are precisely what they are to prompt us to trust him more.

If everything were perfect from our perspective, we wouldn't need God. Our circumstances, especially when they seem too complicated or sparse, are the ideal soil for spiritual growth and maturity. We can trust that while God is at work in our circumstances, he is also at work in us. God is sovereign over our affairs; he will use them as he sees fit: as roadblocks to hold or stop us, propellants to move us forward, or directional signs to point us where we should be going. Rosemary Jensen, a past Executive Director of Bible Study Fellowship, once said that if God has presented a door of opportunity, we should push on it gently. If it opens, we should walk through it. However, if we find a door that we must beat down, it is probably not the door God would have us walk through.

We must be sensitive to our circumstances. Is God using them to direct our path? Probably. He may say stop, wait, turn here, turn around, or move full-speed ahead, using our circumstances to direct us. God is not a God of chaos but order; he will lead us along an orderly path. Though it may not seem straight or the fastest, it will be orderly.

God may also use our circumstances as pruning shears. God is faithful in showing us the physical, emotional, and spiritual clutter in our lives that manifests in our service. Letting him prune away the disorder is not easy, but how can we move forward in our service to God if there is a disorder in our spirit? With his pruning, God removes habits that feed chaos, nurtures unresolved emotional issues, and gets rid of spiritual garbage that prevents us from trusting him completely. He prunes our lives in and through our circumstances, because we live in our circumstances.

Just like any gardener, God doesn't take the grapevine out of the garden to prune it; he prunes it where it is—where it is planted and growing. God prunes in the circumstances. When something needs to go, God doesn't use long-handled loppers; he holds the branch close and cuts it in the perfect place. The branches that bear fruit are not left alone either; they are also pruned so they will yield more fruit. God is intimately involved in every detail and every circumstance of our lives and our service—for our good and his glory. He is not random in his actions; he is meticulous and orderly.

While God is at work in our circumstances, so must we be as we seek to know and do his will. We must be actively at work doing what we believe he would have us do, without scheming to make things happen according to our agenda or within our schedule—that would be the beating down doors scenario. Scheming is not trusting God; it is faithlessness. Scheming says to God that he must not only put the shears down, but that we demand to pick them up ourselves. Scheming is both a result of and a cause of chaos, which may initially seem to speed things up or allow us to get what we want, but it will eventually thwart God's blessings and provision. God's plans and desires for us will align with our circumstances, enabling us to move confidently forward into the service, leadership, or ministry he calls us to.

The Presence of Peace

When God's plan aligns with his Word, and our circumstances are favorable (perhaps not likable or perfect, but circumstances within which we can do the work), we can step into his plan with confident assurance. As we do, we will know immediately that we are on the right track because we will experience a peace that can only be explained with the knowledge that God is in it. This is the power of God's Word. *Do not be anxious about anything, but in everything by prayer and supplication with thanksgiving let your requests be made known to God. And the peace of God, which surpasses all understanding, will guard your hearts and your minds in Christ Jesus* (Philippians 4:6-7).

It is inconceivable to think that the Twelve, when told to seat the multitude of five thousand men plus women and children, didn't immediately experience some excitement along with some nervous energy. Yet, amidst the potential volatility of such a large crowd turning on them (because no one knew what was coming next), I'm sure there was also great peace. Jesus was in control. Jesus was speaking. There was enough room for everyone, and everything was orderly. Something was about to happen!

Having peace does not preclude excitement or anticipation. Peace is not the absence of conflict, but it is the absence of scheming. It doesn't mean we aren't fearful, but it does mean we trust God. Peace is not fatalism; it is hope. I believe the peace experienced on that hillside was the kind that comes when we know we are acting in complete obedience to the Lord's instruction, entirely in alignment with his words, and fully trusting our God. This is the same peace we experience when we are in harmony with

God and know he is present. And it was probably enormously invigorating.

When the apostle Paul was a prisoner on a ship to Rome in the middle of a storm that had been raging for two weeks, he heard the words of Jesus, remained calm, and encouraged the sailors. Paul's circumstances were far from perfect or peaceful, but God was at work in that storm and in the life of every man on board. Jesus' instructions for Paul aligned with God's character and with Paul's tumultuous circumstances. Paul obeyed, and therefore, he had peace: not just any peace, but peace that surpasses the understanding of anyone who has not experienced it. The peace that calms our hearts as it penetrates through every difficulty when we believe what God says will come to pass.

Does this work in real life? Can we clearly and honestly see this alignment? A few years ago, a dear friend wanted to begin a ministry in her church. It was a ministry that she cherished and was perfectly in alignment with God's Word. Her heart was fully committed; she desired to bring honor and glory to God by serving his people; there was no selfish ambition. After praying, she had great peace about moving forward, and everyone praying with and for her agreed. Every door seemed to be opening. So, she approached her pastor. In a stunning turn of events, he declined the use of the building. It seemed everything was in alignment: her circumstances (she had time and passion but needed a host church), the inner peace of obedience (she was ready to move forward), and God's Word (the mission was to minister to women and children). However, her pastor declined the use of the building. Roadblock? Directional Sign? Pruning?

It would have been easy enough to go to another church. She had friends who supported her and were members at other churches, but when her pastor said, "No," her peace also left. She knew she could not scheme to make this happen, and being a godly woman, she decided to pray and ask

God what she should do. God graciously revealed to her that there was unconfessed sin in her heart; broken relationships needed reconciliation before she could establish the ministry.

God used her circumstances to reveal her heart. Aligning our hearts with God's heart is infinitely more important than any service we might accomplish for him. We must yield to God's ordering of our circumstances to achieve structure in our lives.

All three components must align: God's Word, our circumstances, and the inner peace of obedience. God will use any misalignment of these three to prompt us to pause and further seek his will. We must not forge ahead if he is not leading.

When God's Word, our circumstances, and the inner peace of an obedient heart align, we can move confidently, knowing that God is directing our lives and our service. We can trust that when God calls us to a ministry, there is a plan that rises above the chaos, disorder, and confusion of the world, bringing us peace and harmony.

To become godly leaders who feed Jesus' sheep with certainty, we must believe **_that there is no confusion in God._** *To overcome any uncertainty in our leadership, it is necessary to repent of the chaos, disorder, and confusion we live in and not excuse ourselves as "just who we are," but trust God as he leads us through his Word and our circumstances, bringing us the inner peace of obedience.*

Questions for Discussion

1. What do you fear most: stepping outside God's will for you or stepping into it?

2. How well do you know your Shepherd's voice? What is your plan for tuning your ear to hear his voice?

3. Is there a command God has given you that you have not obeyed? Why haven't you?

4. What is your intentional plan for spending time in God's Word?

5. In what circumstances do you find it difficult to trust God? Why?

6. What specific things would you say create chaos or disorder in your spiritual life? Your physical life? Your emotional life?

7. What chaos is God pruning from your life so that you might be more fruitful for him?

8. Have you ever felt the need to scheme to help God along? How did that work for you?

9. Describe a time when you felt the peace that passes understanding. How did God use that to direct your life?

Chapter 8

Pray Continually

Rejoice always, pray without ceasing, give thanks in all circumstances; for this is the will of God in Christ Jesus for you.
1 Thessalonians 5:16-18

God tells us—commands us—to rejoice always, pray continually, and give thanks in all circumstances. As God's people, we can trust that whatever our circumstances are, they are precisely what God would have them be, even when they are anything but what *we* would have them be.

As leaders, we must trust that God knows exactly what is going on in our lives; we are to rejoice, pray, and give thanks because he knows what is best for us. He knows when to change or reorder our circumstances, and he knows when to leave things just as they are. He knows when to rescue us and when to allow us to persevere and endure. God is fully aware at every moment when we need less or more of anything. Godly leaders understand and accept that what they have is perfect for the moment—that is the key to persevering through hard times. God is good all the time. Nothing is random, fate, or arbitrary. And nothing is a coincidence—not for us, not for the Twelve on that hillside, and certainly not for Jesus.

There was a multitude of hungry people and only one little boy's dinner. Before Jesus did anything, he prayed. Jesus prayed over a meager basket of food, giving thanks for what he had; he did not ask God to change the circumstances or send the people home. He prayed about what he had, and God blessed it. *And taking the five loaves and the two fish, he looked up to heaven and said a blessing* (Mark 6:41a).

Some other versions say *he gave thanks.* Thanks? For what? For the people? For the little bit of food? For the Twelve? For the moment? For all he had? For what he didn't have? How hard was it to be grateful for what he had when what he had seemed tragically insufficient?

It is challenging to thank God for what we don't have, for what God has not yet given or has withheld. Do we even pray those kinds of prayers? I will confess that I rarely do. The darkness of ingratitude can be oppressively thick when my heart is shrouded in what I think are unmet needs. When my prayers are repetitive with "I need" and "Please give me," rejoicing seems foreign. Perhaps that is the problem—our hearts and vision dictate whether we are grateful rather than allowing gratitude to lead us into prayers of thanksgiving and rejoicing. Like the Twelve, we need training to overcome dreadful grumbling and develop a perpetual attitude of gratitude, no matter the circumstances.

God understands our situation far more than we do, and he knows what we need before we ask. We've already learned that he will provide what he requires of us, so it seems reasonable that God knows whatever we perceive as lacking is probably unnecessary. We may not feel we have all we need, but he still commands us to pray with thanksgiving. And rejoicing. And praise. Sometimes, we must let prayer direct our emotions rather than allowing our emotions to direct our prayers.

Gratitude is a choice. We are responsible for expressing our gratitude in prayer as we exercise our faith in God's omniscience and proclaim our trust in him. As we pray (asking for what we need with gratitude for what we have), we also lead others to trust God. On the contrary, dictating to God what we want him to do—as if he is obligated to provide what we assume we cannot do without—teaches others to pray similarly. We lead by our actions and words in whatever capacity we serve.

What do your prayers sound like? Maybe it's time we listen to our prayers. Is there grumbling and complaining? Do you pour out your needs, reminding God of how he's overlooked you and telling him what he should do? And after you pray, do you wait to see what, if anything, he sends your way? How, if at all, he reengineers your circumstances? And what if he doesn't? Will you continue to trust him and submit to his sovereignty in and over your circumstances?

When we pray, we can gratefully rejoice that God is with us and has his hand upon us. We celebrate that he meets us with love, guidance, protection, sanctification, and provision. God commands us to cast all our cares, needs, and *anxieties on him because he cares for [us]* (1 Peter 5:7), which we do in prayer. We also pray to offer him thanks for everything he has already given us. Everything—what we see, what we have, and what we don't see and don't have. Then we wait. We leave everything to God and wait to see what he will or will not do.

What do we do while we wait? What attitude should we have? An attitude of complete trust. When all we see seems pitifully little and we choose to bow before God in prayer, God sees our trusting heart instead of a whining and complaining spirit. God is faithful; he *will* provide all we need—it may not be what we think we need, but it is precisely what God knows we need. We can trust that in his perfect timing, the One who sees everything and has every resource in the universe at his disposal will be generous and giving beyond what we deserve. In the meantime, we can be grateful for what we have, because gratitude is his will for us in all circumstances.

The most significant indicator of how we pray is not how we ask for what we think we need or don't need, but how we see God and perceive the Person of God. How do you see God? How do you perceive his role in your life? In your prayers?

Do we think of God as simply the transcendent Creator of the universe who is far off, so busy taking care of essential things that he has no time for us or our circumstances? If that is our perspective, we do our best with what we have. We consider that we are on our own to devise the plans and means to secure what we need, and that there is no need to pray because God is too distracted to hear us anyway. Also, because we are busy securing every resource we need, there is no room or reason for gratitude. We reason that God doesn't care about us or our prayers; he's too busy running the universe. If this is how we see God, we cannot be grateful, because we do not recognize the reality of who God is or his involvement in the day-to-day of our lives.

For some of us, God is like a genie in a lamp; we think that if we rub the side of the lamp—do the things we're supposed to, following the format we've been taught—we'll get whatever we ask. Let's see, what is the formula? How do I polish the lamp? Do I begin with ACTS—Adoration, Confession, Thanksgiving, Supplication? Or is it CATS, with Confession first? Or is it PRAY—Praise, Repent, Ask, and, what was the Y for?, Yield? Yourself? If we fail to get the proper order, will God hear us? Have I been polishing with the wrong cloth? Rubbing in the wrong direction? Could that be why my wishes, er, I mean prayers, were not granted? There is very little gratitude in our prayers when we feel we've earned whatever we've received because we utilized the correct formula. There is little gratitude because we think God is obligated to us if we get the procedure right.

Or maybe we think God is like Santa Claus. We spend a little time sitting on his knee, dictating to him our list of desires (of course, we put our needs first, and then, if there's time, we'll cover the wants), then we behave like good little Christian boys and girls and stay off the naughty list until he gives us what we've asked. There is very little gratitude in our hearts as we give him our perfunctory "thank you" (we were always taught to say "thank you" for our presents) because we believe we earned his gifts with our behavior. We'll be grateful only until we need or want something else.

Perhaps we think God is like a benevolent uncle or wealthy grandpa; as long as we visit and chat with him occasionally, he'll remember us and give us what we want; after all, he can afford it. We bring our list, sit in our favorite comfy chair, and sip our beverage of choice while we mindlessly think, write, or sometimes speak our prayers; then we get up, walk away, and check off our visit for the day. There is no gratitude because, for the most part, we don't even know when or if our prayers have been answered. After all, we were chatting. It would not be nice to make specific requests. And maybe God owes us for spending a little time with him while we pay our respects.

Is any of this real prayer? Is this what it looks like to beseech the Almighty? These prayers are equivalent to online shopping; we scan the list, add it to the cart, click buy, and then wait for the delivery. There is power in online shopping; there is a guarantee that a package or a sack of groceries will appear on the front step in short order. There is no power in the "prayers" as they are delineated above. That is not how Jesus prayed; it is not what the Twelve witnessed that prompted them to ask Jesus to teach them to pray. And I don't think that is what God desires when he tells us to come before him in prayer, in all circumstances, all the time.

So, what is prayer? What does it look like? How do we do it? How often should we pray? First, I'm not an authority on prayer (and I confess, I have prayed in all of the ways mentioned above, so I'm probably an authority on how *not* to pray); nevertheless, I know that prayer is not easy. If it were, we'd do it more often. Prayer is warfare. When we pray, we go into battle, setting up a boundary and claiming the land for God, and the evil one will not be happy about it. Therefore, we must pray armed with humility, worship, and reverence for God; probably not the weapons most of us think we need to fight evil, but they are powerful when used in prayer.

Prayer, at its simplest, is a conversation with God. It is similar to a conversation between a child and a parent, a soldier and his commanding officer, or a student and a teacher. The lesser submits to the greater; therefore, prayer requires humility. The essence of prayer is going before God and saying, "Dad, I can't do this alone. I don't have what it takes. I am not strong, wise, good, or resourceful enough. I need help, and you are the only One who can sufficiently help me. Please help me." If we could do things independently, have what it takes, and be strong, wise, good, and resourceful enough, we wouldn't need to pray.

Prayer is worship. When we pray, we submit ourselves before and to God, acknowledging his sovereignty over all things and our inability to live apart from his sustenance. Prayer is worship that glorifies God's character and attributes and declares that he alone is worthy of praise, honor, and exaltation. Praying forces us to confess that we are not God—to recognize our place, get off the little thrones of our hearts, and exercise the privilege and responsibility of yielding to God's authority and wisdom. Prayer reminds us that God alone is worthy of our reverent love, adoration, and allegiance.

Prayer Is Personal, Private, and Public

Prayer is personal. When we pray, we have God's undivided attention and are free to divulge our fears, weaknesses, heartaches, desires, deepest yearnings, hopes, disappointments, frustrations, and our sincerest concerns to him without fear of judgment or rejection. When we go into our Father's presence in prayer, we open our hearts for his loving inspection and acknowledge that what he sees there is true and accurate. Where there is sin, we confess and repent of it, knowing that God *is faithful and just to forgive us our sins and to cleanse us from all unrighteousness* (1 John 1:9). Where there is unforgiveness, we forgive. Where there is a root of bitterness, we work with God to dig it out. Where there is rejoicing, we share it with him. No heartache or rejoicing, failure or victory, loss or gain is complete until we share it with God. In prayer, we pour out every bit of our independence that strives for control over our little personal kingdoms and ask God to fill us with his Holy Spirit, which leads us deeper into the complete dependence we need.

Prayer is private. In prayer, God uncovers our deepest secrets, and as we confess our guilt, he removes our shame. He dismantles every stronghold, and we find acceptance for who we truly are rather than who we project to be. In prayer, we confidently *draw near to the throne of grace, that we may receive mercy and find grace to help in time of need* (Hebrews 4:16), and we remember who Jesus is—not our assistant, but our Lord. We don't ask him to come alongside our plans and bless our ideas; we submit to him as the Lord over our plans and ideas. In prayer, our facades are washed away, our notions are set aside, our will is aligned with God, and we gratefully thank him for loving us and using us for his kingdom work.

While prayer is private and personal, it can also be public. Public prayer is the opportunity to join our brothers and sisters in the corporate worship of our King and lay our needs before him. Public prayer allows a community of individuals to unite before the Father in the body of Christ in one accord, seeking his will and his glory. Corporate prayer is a powerful privilege for the family of believers; it is never an opportunity for grandstanding or speaking so that others hear eloquent words. Joining with others to pray is a beautiful time to knit the family of God together in heartfelt gratitude as we present our deficiencies and celebrate his sufficiencies so that we see the hand of God in our circumstances more gloriously.

Prayer is also an attitude. God tells us to pray continually and in all things, but what does that look like? Should we sit in our prayer closets all day, every day, praying? Do we pray rather than work? I don't think so. I think it means that prayer is an ongoing conversation with God. Every day, we should be in continual communication with the Almighty. We are to be so connected with him that he is always on our minds and hearts wherever we are and whatever we are doing. God longs for us to run everything by him and seek his will in all things, trusting not in our understanding but acknowledging his character and way so that we are careful to walk in it in everyday life decisions, not just the major ones. An attitude of prayer is a way of life, and it must be the way of our service.

Leading in an attitude of prayer includes removing distractions and sitting with God individually and with our teams for regular periods of consistent, concerted prayer. When we come before God, we must remember whom we are approaching. In the Old Testament, no one dared approach God willy-nilly, not even the high priest. Moses shared the Lord's instructions, *"And be ready for the third day. For on the third day the Lord will come down on Mount Sinai in the sight of all the people. And you shall set limits for the people all around, saying, 'Take care not to go up into the mountain or touch the edge of it. Whoever touches the mountain shall be put to death'"* (Exodus 19:11–12). *And the Lord said to Moses, "Tell Aaron your brother not to come at any time into the Holy Place inside the veil, before the mercy seat that is on the ark, so that he may not die"* (Leviticus 16:2).

Fortunately, we are not living in Old Testament times when a priest's intercession was required before coming to God; we are living in the day of the *new covenant* (Hebrews 9:15). *We have a great high priest who has passed through the heavens, Jesus, the Son of God* (Hebrews 4:14), therefore God no longer requires that we have a physical, human high priest to intercede for us. Jesus offered the perfect sacrifice, *once for all* (Hebrews

9:12), giving us direct, personal access to the Father. However, I don't think we should throw the baby out with the bathwater and take this precious privilege for granted. Dare we saunter into the throne room of the Almighty without a care? Well, yes, we can go into God's presence whenever we want and pray directly to God. But we can go only because the precious blood of Jesus opened the way. We must never fail to be aware of the cost to God that allows us both this extraordinary privilege and great responsibility.

As God's children, because of the blood of Jesus, we have the great privilege, honor, and responsibility to come before God in prayer at all times for all things. Therefore, as his servant leaders, we must remember our King's great sacrifice, which gave us this privilege, and offer him his due by coming before him humbly, contritely, regularly, and submissively surrendered. Our example of humble prayer will train those we serve to recognize that we all bow before Jesus.

As we come with awe, wonder, reverence, adoration, and worship, our privilege should propel us into his presence with heartfelt gratitude throughout every day. We should come often and linger long because we love him and want to do great things for him and serve his people well. It is to our advantage to spend time with him, for it is in prayer that we align our will with God's will and find strength for the day. In prayer, we find healing salve for our wounds, submit our requests to God, and are equipped to do the work God has for us. Prayer should compel us toward godly service, and service should compel us to pray.

If prayer is talking with God, who exactly am I speaking with? God the Father? God the Son, Jesus? Or God the Holy Spirit? Prayer involves all three Persons of the Trinity. We talk to the Father as a child whom the Father loves and has invited into his presence. We are welcomed into the Father's presence because of the blood of Jesus, the Son. Jesus paid the penalty for our sins, and his blood cleanses us from all unrighteousness. And it is the Holy Spirit who *bears witness with our spirit that we are children of God* (Romans 8:16). *Likewise the Spirit helps us in our weakness. For we do not know what to pray for as we ought, but the Spirit himself intercedes for us with groanings too deep for words. And he who searches hearts knows what is the mind of the Spirit, because the Spirit intercedes for the saints according to the will of God* (Romans 8:26-27). Prayer is a privilege. As we avail ourselves of this precious gift, we find that it unleashes the power of God in our lives and our leadership—the power we need to serve faithfully.

We Must Be Grateful
for What We Have and for What We Don't Have

As God's people who love God and desire to serve his people, we are to pray with thanksgiving as Jesus did—thanksgiving for what we have and for what we do not have. The Bible tells us that God knows our needs even before we ask; therefore, some may ask, Why pray? We pray because prayer is the means God ordained to accomplish his ends. Jesus himself said, *"Your Father knows what you need before you ask him. Pray then like this: Our Father in heaven, hallowed be your name, your kingdom come, your will be done, on earth as it is in heaven. Give us this day our daily bread, and forgive us our debts, as we also have forgiven our debtors. And lead us not into temptation, but deliver us from evil"* (Matthew 6:8b-13).

When the Twelve asked Jesus to teach them how to pray, Jesus gave the pattern that our prayers should reflect. His example is not a formula, but a way of praying that acknowledges the Father's sovereignty, majesty, and glory and recognizes our complete dependence on God. If we want to serve and feed others in a way that honors God, our prayers must continually flow from submissive hearts in full surrender to God.

The Bible teaches us to rejoice in all things and pray with thanksgiving. It is easy to pray with gratitude for what we have received, but what about the things we have not yet received, or perhaps never will? We can always be grateful for what we do not have because, even when God does not see fit to give us something we want, we can trust him. God is all-wise; he knows what is best for us. And he knows what he is doing in, for, and through us, including what is best to withhold from us and for how long. Unfortunately, we tend to grow dissatisfied and ungrateful when we focus on what we don't have. When, in our prayers, we repetitively ask for the same thing, we struggle to reconcile: Am I trying to convince God to give me what I want? By my asking, am I refusing his "no," or am I being persistent?

Jesus taught the disciples to persevere in prayer and not give up; however, how do we know whether the answer is "no" or "not yet"? Can we? Are we not receiving because it isn't God's time, or the answer is no, or is there another reason? Maybe we need to check our hearts and attitudes. James, the brother of Jesus, teaches us, *But let him ask in faith, with no doubting, for the one who doubts is like a wave of the sea that is driven and tossed by the wind. For that person must not suppose that he will receive anything from the Lord; he is a double-minded man, unstable in all his ways* (James 1:6-8). Is James saying we should not expect to receive anything from the Lord if we pray with doubts? He later states, *You ask and do not receive, because you ask wrongly, to spend it on your passions* (James 4:3). So, we have to worry about our doubts *and* our motives? And yet, Mark teaches us, *Whatever you ask in prayer, believe that you have received it, and it will be yours* (Mark 11:24). This can all be so confusing.

We know we sometimes have doubts. We know we sometimes have wrong motives. We know we cannot name it and claim it. But what if we get it all right—we believe, have the best reasons, and do our best not to doubt—but still don't get what we're asking for? At those times, we must remember that God is good and has the wisdom to know what is best for us. He can and does say "no," especially if that "no" is what will most grow our faith. Some of our most significant "Thank you" prayers are prayers we've prayed when we realize that the best thing God ever did for us was to say "no."

God often changes our perspective as we pray, aligning our vision and understanding with his. There was a time when I struggled to submit to a supervisor because she and I seemed to be on different pages about too many things. She didn't understand me and assigned wrong motives to almost everything I did or asked about. I wanted a loving and encouraging supervisor; it was challenging to be grateful for the one I had. There were many times, more than I'd like to admit, when I prayed and asked God to reassign her or me. Numerous times, I just wanted to quit, and I told God that. But he didn't let me leave, and he didn't change my supervisor. However, he did change my vision and understanding.

God kept reminding me, as I prayed, that he was in control, not only of my leadership role but also of my supervisor's assignment and the entire organization. God was working mightily in me. He was not giving me what I wanted, but what I needed, and he was withholding what would not have benefited me. This supervisor taught me a lot about leadership—how to lead, and, especially, how not to lead. I learned that I must submit to my God-appointed leaders even when I may not like their leadership style.

God was patient with me; he knew my heart needed realignment with his. It took time, but now, I am grateful she was assigned to me. And, most likely, every person I've led or served since has benefitted from my experience with that supervisor. God was training me through what I didn't have and thought I wanted, but he knew what I needed, and he gave it to me. I learned to be open to God's leading and direction as I pray, and to be grateful for what he provides and for what he withholds. Often, we can learn more from what is withheld than what we receive.

If we believe we have insufficient resources to do the work God has called us to, and if we think, behave, and pray as if we have nothing to be thankful for, or worse yet, complain and grumble about what we do or don't have, we might as well consider ourselves failing in our service. There is always something to be thankful for. God is always at work for good in the lives of those who love him. If we cannot see what he is doing, it doesn't mean he is not there; it means our vision is clouded. As we pray, God will cleanse our lens and correct our vision.

So we can always begin by thanking him for who he is: God Almighty! And for what we know to be true: he is always good, he is always at work, he is perfectly accomplishing his purpose, and his purposes can never be thwarted by anyone or anything. For that, we must be thankful! We must seek to see beyond our perceived needs and thank him for all he has provided.

When we are ungrateful, we believe we are entitled to or responsible for what we have accomplished or accumulated; therefore, we deserve all the credit and the accompanying accolades. The absence of gratitude is pride. When we attribute our success to our uniqueness, resourcefulness, abilities, intelligence, personality, or whatever else we want to think we have created, we pat ourselves on the back and ignore God.

Pride makes us self-reliant and fools us into believing we are self-sufficient, telling us to go our way and to do our own thing. When we are prideful, we do not accept failure and blame God for what has not been provided or what we have not accomplished. When we have everything we think we need, pride tells us we don't need God. When we think we don't need God, we rarely, if ever, pray. Why should we? Instead, grumbling and complaining take over. We will not abound in thankfulness until we realize that all we have, even if it appears as meager and paltry as a little boy's lunch in the face of a hungry multitude, is a gracious gift from God.

Jesus, taking what he had, prayed. Jesus knew what he would do; he always had a plan, and I believe he was training the Twelve to rely on, place their trust in, and be grateful for God's perfectly timed provision. Why did they need to learn this lesson? Why do we? Because if we don't, we will become grumblers and complainers and forfeit contentment. Without contentment, we will abandon our service. It is easy to quit when we feel we are working alone with too few provisions.

When we don't have answers for the difficult questions or can't secure the means to help ourselves or anyone else, when the circumstances of our leadership and service overwhelm us and darkness seems to be setting in as the problems of the day engulf us, when we have pitiful little left with which to serve, it is then that we must remember who God is. He is good, kind, generous, all-wise, trustworthy, gracious, and the extravagant giver of every perfect gift.

God does not promise everything will work out as we hope or even that he will not give us more than we can bear, but he does promise that when struggles bring us to the end of our resources and ourselves, he will help us. And he is sufficient. *For we do not want you to be unaware, brothers, of the affliction we experienced in Asia. For we were so utterly burdened beyond our strength that we despaired of life itself. Indeed, we felt that we had received the sentence of death. But that was to make us rely not on ourselves but on God who raises the dead* (2 Corinthians 1:8-9).

Circumstances can rob us of our joy in service, or they can multiply our gratitude. Jesus prayed and asked God to bless the food, and we know what happened next. We must take what we have, however small and limited, and receive it as a gift from God for this day, for his purpose, and thank him. Oh, how our hearts overflow with thanksgiving when we recognize and acknowledge God's gracious abundance in everything. Gratitude teaches us contentment.

Jeremiah Burroughs, a preacher in the 17th century, defined contentment as "That sweet, inward, quiet, gracious frame of spirit which freely submits to and delights in God's wise and fatherly disposition in every condition."[1] This contentment was epitomized in Jesus' example on that hillside. He was sweet: He cared for the crowds, teaching and healing them. His inward frame of spirit was quiet: His words or demeanor had no panic, hurry, or fear. He was gracious: He tended to the Twelve's training and the multitude's needs. He freely submitted to and delighted in God's wise and fatherly disposition, thanking him for what he had provided.

As we see God's provision as wise and fatherly, we become grateful children. When we trust his provision in every condition, we are unafraid to be generous with what we have. That doesn't mean we cannot ask for a miracle because, as we all know, a miracle was needed that evening in Galilee, and a miracle was provided. Of course, we should ask for miracles and expect them. Do we not have because we do not ask? Are we persevering in our asking? Have we decided that God's "no" or his "wait" are reasons for grumbling? The more grateful we are, the more we will see all God has provided.

Relying on the character of God rather than on what we can or cannot see assures that we will never be disappointed. God always provides what is best for us; he is faithful, and we can trust him. The key to contentment is gratefully accepting that what we have been given is precisely what God intends for us to have right now. Contentment becomes our default attitude as we take that truth and live rejoicing in what we have rather than

---

1. Burroughs, Jeremiah, *The Rare Jewel of Christian Contentment*. Banner of Truth Trust, First published 1648, reprinted 2013. Pg. 19

miserably dwelling on what we don't have. Thanksgiving and contentment go hand in hand.

Our circumstances should never affect our thankfulness; thankfulness should always be our attitude, despite the circumstances. If we often feel discontented, overwhelmed, frustrated, helpless, hopeless, taken for granted, or harboring negativity, could it be because we've failed to practice thanksgiving? We will experience joy in our Father's provision as we count our blessings. If we are not practicing gratitude, we will miss the joy of seeing what God is doing as we try to serve others, oblivious to all God has provided. Godly servants are thankful leaders. We have the words of God to feast on and the character of God to sustain us; we will not starve. Gratitude will empower us.

To become godly leaders who feed Jesus' sheep with grateful hearts we must make it a habit **to pray with gratitude continually in all circumstances.** *We must repent of failing to trust that God knows and always provides all that we need. As we practice gratitude, we will overcome the fatigue of grumbling and discontent, allowing us to persevere in our leadership.*

Questions for Discussion

1. For what (in your service/leadership) are you thankful today?

2. Are you living in contentment?

3. What vision of God directs your prayers?

4. If God gave you everything you asked for, would any life (besides your own) change? How?

5. Are you thankful for what God has not yet (or perhaps will never) give you? List some things you are praying for that have been withheld from you. Will you pause to thank God for his wisdom and timing?

6. How might your leadership differ if you had received all you prayed for? How is it better because you've received what God has given you? How is it better that you have not received everything you requested?

7. Are you generous with what you've been given?

8. Does thankfulness drive your attitude, or does your attitude drive your thankfulness?

9. List all the things God has given you for which you've failed to be thankful.

10. What part of the definition of contentment do you most identify with? What do you most struggle with?

Chapter 9

Dependent Distributors

Now to him who is able to do far more abundantly than all that we ask or think, according to the power at work within us, to him be glory in the church and in Christ Jesus throughout all generations, forever and ever. Amen.
Ephesians 3:20-21

It cannot be stressed enough that our service is not about us. It's also not about our success or failure, or our image or reputation. Our service must always be all about God. We are the pots God created for his purpose. *We are his workmanship, created in Christ Jesus for good works, which God prepared beforehand, that we should walk in them* (Ephesians 2:10). We belong to God, and God has the prerogative where and how to utilize us for his good purpose. We are most blessed that he uses us to serve his sheep, and we should always be amazed that he has granted us this privilege.

Amazingly, as we serve, we are blessed; in our service, others receive blessings; and through our service, God sanctifies us—all for his glory. Our service to others doesn't promote ourselves; it promotes God. We are billboards to declare his grace and his glory—he saved us by his grace, and he has work for us to do that will bring him glory. *Let your light shine before others, so that they may see your good works and give glory to your Father who is in heaven* (Matthew 5:16). We must always be amazed at what he can and often does through us! Unique, powerful things! More than we can ask or imagine. To experience that magnificence, let your light shine by lovingly and joyfully doing the tasks he assigns you, just like the Twelve did. It is impossible to know everything that happened that day, but let's try to imagine it.

By the time everyone was seated on the ground, the Twelve knew they were not the main attraction. It was not their winsome personalities that drew the crowds initially, nor their previous notoriety of healing or casting out demons that kept them there. No, the people came to see Jesus and get what they could. As the evening approached and the events began to unfold, I imagine there was excitement and anticipation about what Jesus would do next. Every eye was looking at Jesus. All attention focused on him: The Son of God and the Son of Man. What was he going to do?

No one knew what to expect. They'd heard about Jesus enough to know that the laws of physics or nature did not bind him, and he had fully taken control of the moment. They knew Jesus was capable of the spectacular, the unexpected, and the thrill, and they all came to see just that. Would he let them down? Would he amaze? No one knew what would happen next, but everyone knew to look to Jesus. *And taking the five loaves and the two fish, he looked up to heaven and said a blessing over them. Then he broke the loaves and gave them to the disciples to set before the crowd* (Luke 9:16).

Conservatively, ten thousand hungry people were sitting in groups on that hillside. If each group averaged about seventy-five people, there would have been about 133 groups; that is, about eleven or twelve groups for each disciple. That's a lot of hungry, tired, anxious people spread out over an area at least the size of two football fields, or perhaps larger. Suppose any of the Twelve had entertained an idea of autonomy, working independently of Jesus or each other that evening. Those thoughts would have flown right out the window when they looked at the mass of humanity. This was not a time for independence; it was the time to let go of self-sufficiency and unite in service, mission, and obedience. This was the time to be united in Jesus. They were learning to lean into Jesus in complete dependence.

Who was in the crowd that evening? I imagine there were grandmas and grandpas, older people who had walked and perhaps stood all day and were now ready to sit, eat, and rest. There were young moms, exhausted from corralling toddlers, kissing skinned knees, nursing infants, and comforting the sleep-deprived. Young men and fathers, who were anxious to know the truth about this celebrity pastor to whom they had led their families. There were those who, just hours earlier, had experienced healing and rejoiced in the hope of more days with their loved ones. There were curious students whose lives were changing as they heard from the Master Teacher. However, most of those present were there for the circus. And now, what they would see next was utterly unknown, so they sat down, listened, and waited. That is always a good thing to do when Jesus is present.

Godly Leaders Wait on Jesus

Do you wonder what they talked about in their groups? It was getting late; they should have been on their way, yet something compelled them to stay. At that moment, every person appeared to be united in a degree of expectation centered on Jesus, and everyone was waiting on him.

What does it look like to wait on Jesus? Every Christian today is ultimately waiting for Jesus to return to this world and live among us, for him to return to judge and reign over the world. We wait because we believe in his promises. As servant leaders, we know to wait on Jesus when we don't know what the next moment holds because, without him leading the way, we don't know where we are going or what we will do when we get there, much like the Twelve. Waiting, therefore, is an act of faith grounded in God's promises; the object is Jesus.

We have this faith because God has kept every past promise, and therefore, we know he will keep every promise whose fulfillment is future to us. So, we wait, like the tired, hungry souls on that hillside, with anticipation, hope, excitement, and complete dependence upon God's character and Person.

The Twelve waited because there was nothing else they could do; the situation was beyond their ability and out of their hands. They were prepared to do only that which Jesus told them to do. Waiting is an act of surrender that admits we can do nothing apart from Jesus and declares that we are wholly dependent on the faithful One. The Twelve were surrendered to Jesus, the One who held the moment, because they knew and trusted him.

Everyone stayed. To wait means to be firm even when things seem impossible or improbable. As Christians, we stand firm because we stand upon the Solid Rock. Waiting is the vehicle, or conduit, through which we receive the reward for overcoming independence and leaning fully on God. And what is the reward? It is seeing God at work in his perfect way and time.

What would the Twelve have missed if one of them had decided not to wait? If one had independently stepped up and told Jesus there was no time to wait, and had sent the people home or tried to find food on his own? The best plan is to dependently wait for God's perfect plan to unfold in his way and time. What do we mean by waiting on God? We tend to think waiting is what we do while passing the time until someone who is late shows up. But God is not slow; he isn't late for an appointment, hasn't forgotten us, isn't out there in the cosmos trying to devise a plan for our predicament, and he surely isn't trying to figure out where to get the resources he needs. God knows what he is doing and what he will do. He has all the time in eternity to accomplish his predetermined plan and is using that time for his good purposes and glory. What we mean by waiting is that we will stay put until God tells us to move. We won't scheme, plot, push forward, or devise separate plans. We will not rush ahead of God or be impatient. Our waiting tells God, "I'm content with your timing, and I trust your plans." So, we wait.

However, we are not idle as we wait; we use that time to pray, trust, and do whatever God wants. We wait with expectation, hope, confidence, and excitement rather than impatience, despair, or fear because we know that God is at work in the waiting. *In the morning, Lord, you hear my voice; in the morning I lay my requests before you and wait expectantly* (Psalm 5:3 NIV). *Indeed, none who wait for you shall be put to shame* (Psalm 25:3a). *Wait for the Lord; be strong and let your heart take courage; wait for the Lord!* (Psalm 27:14). *Our soul waits for the Lord; he is our help and our shield. For our heart is glad in him, because we trust in his holy name* (Psalm 33:20-21).

Jesus trained every person on that hillside to wait on him. He showed them that in him, there is no room for independence. He is the all-sufficient One. Sometimes, that is a lesson that we must learn again and again. I was involved in a ministry that was good at waiting on God. We prayed for funding, volunteers, everything, no matter how long it took, we waited patiently and God always came through for us, often just in the nick of time. But one year, things looked dire, and we didn't wait on God. We ran full speed ahead in our independence because, after all, we had a ministry to run, and God was not meeting our schedule. We followed the school calendar, and by the end of May, we wanted all our ducks in a row to begin fresh in September.

However, that fateful year, one of the directors resigned early in the summer, and by August, we didn't have anyone on board to take her place. Desperate and in bondage to the calendar, the ministry leader emailed the staff, asking us to pray for a director. Great idea! When all else fails, pray! (Well, maybe we should have thought of that before, but our failure is now an illustration in a leadership book on how not to serve independently of God.) A staff member who received the email quickly volunteered to step into the director role; after all, she had the time and heart for the ministry, she loved God, she wanted to serve his people, and we had the need.

However, did she have the call from God? The ministry leader acted quickly and moved to make the volunteer the director. It was a desperately lousy year in the ministry. Everyone suffered: the new director, the leadership, the volunteers, and those we served. It was as if we were a rudderless ship on a stormy sea.

Should we have waited a bit longer? Would God, in his perfection, have provided the perfect director? What if he didn't? What if God's plan for the ministry was different from ours? We will never know. He let us plummet down the hill of independence in a wagon made of impatience and fear, doing what we thought we needed to do; then he let us suffer the consequences of not waiting on him. After crash-landing—bruised, battered, and in pain and despair—we turned to God in prayerful repentance. All of us—the director, the ministry leader, the volunteers, and those we served—joined together as we confessed our lack of trust and sought forgiveness for not waiting on God. We learned that God's plan and timing are always perfect, and depending on him is the only vehicle for success.

Godly Leaders Are Sacred Go-Betweens

The Twelve had been tested that day as they learned to depend on Jesus; soon, the next lesson began. Jesus handed them the bread and fish; they knew to distribute whatever they received from Jesus. We all need to learn this lesson: In our leadership or servant roles, we have nothing to distribute; we have nothing worth distributing except that which Jesus gives us. We do not serve independently of Jesus. We have nothing to serve if Jesus hasn't given it to us. Moreover, whatever we receive from Jesus, we must give out. That is our role; we are distributors.

It was getting late, the sun was setting, and the spotlight of all eternity shone brightly on Jesus. I'm sure the Twelve were more than content to reflect that light; I suspect they were overjoyed. That is how it must be in our service. We must be the vehicle through which Jesus' light pierces the darkness of our lost world. We are to be content to work utterly dependent on him. His light is within us, and we have the privilege of letting it shine. We cannot force it to shine, but we can remove everything that hinders it from shining—this is our joy. If your leadership or service is joyless, note whether his light from above radiates through you.

Oswald Chambers refers to Christian workers as "sacred go-betweens." In our servant leadership, we must be so closely identified with the Lord Jesus that his life shines through us. We must give out everything we have received from him: reconciliation, the hope of salvation, restoration, grace, mercy, and love. We must identify so closely with Jesus that people can see beyond our personality, our cleverness, and yes, even our service, and see Jesus. Our purpose is not to bring attention to ourselves or to step into the spotlight of God's glory but to be used by him for his purpose and glory. Our life's aim must be to make God more famous in the world.

God created us for his glory. He has full authority over our lives; in him, as Paul quoted, we *"live and move and have our being"* (Acts 17:28). This does not diminish who we are as individuals. We do not get lost in Jesus; we do not lose our personhood. Quite the opposite, we are exalted in Christ, *glorified with him* (Romans 8:17). We were made by God and for God, and he has *called [us] into the fellowship of his Son* (1 Corinthians 1:9). We have fellowship with our Creator. Therefore, our ultimate purpose is to glorify God; as we do that, we will thoroughly enjoy him. How wonderful is that? Imagine how much the Twelve must have enjoyed Jesus that evening. We are God's workers, his sacred go-betweens, bringing his goodness to everyone he places in our paths. What an astonishing truth:

We are conduits of God's love as we depend entirely upon him. As we serve, wholly dependent upon God, those we serve will feel loved by us, but more importantly, they will know God loves them and will feel *his* love.

This miracle is a brilliant display of God's creativity; Jesus took a bit of bread and fish, broke them, and then created sufficient food to feed thousands with the broken pieces. It is as if the wheat was planted, grown, harvested, ground into flour, and baked into bread all within a nanosecond; only the Creator could do this. If we believe that God is the Creator of all things, and he is, and that Jesus is God incarnate, and he is, then we should have no problem believing that this miracle occurred. And if we believe Jesus is fully capable of miracles, and he is, then we should have no problem depending on him for miracles today. He is, after all, the same Jesus. *In the beginning was the Word, and the Word was with God, and the Word was God. He was in the beginning with God. All things were made through him, and without him was not anything made that was made* (John 1:1-3).

This creative power is the same power displayed at the wedding in Cana when Jesus turned water into wine. The servants' dependence upon Jesus at the wedding is the same as ours must be today. Jesus told them to fill six stone jars with water, so they did. Then he told them to draw some out and take it to the banquet master. They did. When did the water turn into wine? In the pitchers they carried, as they obeyed? Or in the water jars? Who knows. The servants do, and Jesus does. I suspect they looked into the jars and the pitchers. Like the Twelve, the servants were distributors with the fantastic privilege of giving out precisely what the Savior gave them. So. Are. We. How blessed we are to experience the graciousness of God as he includes us in his purposes and plans.

Jesus could have spoken a word, and every belly would have been filled, but instead, he chose to use the Twelve to distribute food to the thousands.

God is self-sufficient—he does not need our help; he can accomplish every ministry with his word, but he has a greater purpose and plan. He chooses to use you and me to feed his people. Our responsibility is to depend on him, do as he tells us, and distribute what he gives us. We were created for God's purpose, not vice versa. We may not understand the situations God puts us in any more than the Twelve did. But, because we know the character of God, we understand that every detail, event, opportunity, and occasion rests perfectly in his hand and will have the exact outcome that God has already prepared for. Just as the Twelve trusted Jesus, so can we.

We are led by the same God as the Twelve. We know he will never let us down or leave us. He knows what we need. He loves us with everlasting love. He is all-powerful, all-knowing, all-wise. And he has given us everything we need for success. *We know that for those who love God all things work together for good, for those who are called according to his purpose* (Romans 8:28). We also know that nothing *will be able to separate us from the love of God in Christ Jesus our Lord* (Romans 8:39). This is the God we can trust—the living God, the one true God. When we know God, we can depend on him and give out whatever he gives us, knowing that we will never run out; there will always be enough.

The way the Twelve distributed what Jesus gave them demonstrated their faith; they didn't stop giving after the first basket was empty, but kept returning for more. In my mind's eye, Jesus' hands were a blur, breaking fish and bread, filling basket after basket. As one basket is filled, lifted, and carried away, an empty basket is placed before him, and a disciple stands and waits, looking to see what Jesus will do. Once that basket is filled and removed, another basket is set before Jesus with another set of eyes on him. Will he keep going? Over and over and over and over, another empty basket is filled, and another one appears as soon as it is taken away. For how long?

Every disciple had to make multiple round trips, carrying full baskets to each group, returning with empty baskets, and going out again.

What was required of the Twelve to return to Jesus on that hillside? Faith? Hope? Obedience? Yes. And yet, there was nothing else they could do. They depended on what Jesus was doing, and for however long he'd do it. As they looked at the multitude, there was no other option but to continue their round trips to Jesus with each empty basket, wait for him to fill it, then carry the basket to the next group and distribute the food. Jesus didn't let them down. Not. One. Time. He will not let us down, either. The resting place of our faith must be in the faithfulness of Jesus.

How much did each basket weigh? How much food did each group require? Each group needed almost twenty pounds of fish (assuming a four-ounce serving per person), and seventy-five rolls would give each group of about seventy-five people a snack. That's twenty-five pounds of food for each trip, and surely each group member was served more than one little four-ounce sandwich. Still, if we consider these minimal numbers, each disciple would have had to make about a dozen trips to Jesus to feed his share of the multitude once; that's over a hundred and thirty empty baskets placed before Jesus. That was a lot of baskets with a lot of food to feed a lot of hungry people. And that required a lot of dependence and a lot of faith.

Godly Leaders Give the Best: Jesus

Dependence on Jesus requires faith. Faith, at its most simple, is belief, and genuine faith acts on what is believed. The Twelve demonstrated their faith in Jesus and their complete dependence on him with every empty basket. But what was the alternative? Imagine the ridiculousness of one disciple saying to a waiting group, "I'm not going to go back up there; Jesus might not fill this basket, so here, let me give you what I have."

What did he have? Platitudes? Empty words of worldly wisdom? Imaginary food? Would any of that fill their hungry stomachs? Would any of that honor the Lord? It is foolish to think that anything we offer is better than what Jesus gives, and yet, how often do we do just that? The only thing anyone had to provide or receive on that hillside came from Jesus. Would there be enough? Yes. Always. That is also all that we have: that which comes from Jesus. Will there be enough? Yes. Always.

In this miracle, Jesus trained everyone there, and now us, to depend on him! Come to Jesus; he will give you what you need to feed those he has placed before you. He will give you and me exactly what and how much we need. Come to him and be satisfied. Come to him in prayer, in Bible study, in fellowship. As servant leaders, we are to come to him and be filled, or we will take empty baskets to the hungriest souls.

We must know our role; we are God's creation—created for his purpose to give glory to him, and we are distributors. We are the pinnacle of God's creation, sacred go-betweens; therefore, we must be sure that when we go out to serve, we do not bring anything with us that could contaminate what Jesus has given us to distribute. We are to wash our spiritual hands—to confess to God the things of the world that have dirtied us—before we try to feed others. *If we confess our sins, he is faithful and just to forgive us our sins and to cleanse us from all unrighteousness* (1 John 1:9). Our hearts must be clean if we are to bring Jesus to those whom we serve. We must leave behind the things of the world that are sullied and dirty before we attempt to serve anyone anything. This means we must repent daily of the things of the world that contaminate us.

We must separate ourselves from things that draw attention away from the gospel of Jesus because, ultimately, what we have to give is Jesus. If we are not giving Jesus or pointing people to Jesus, we are feeding them nothing at best and junk food at worst. It is better to provide them with nothing than to pervert the truth. When we act independently of Jesus, we think junk food (a worldly alternative) somehow equates to what he would have us distribute.

Like the Twelve, we must learn that there is nothing better than what Jesus has provided. We have the gospel; we must distribute it in its fullness. It is enough; *for it is the power of God for salvation to everyone who believes* (Romans 1:16).

The gospel saves lost souls and frees people bound in sin. The gospel provides hope to the hopeless, heals the sick, and feeds the starving. The gospel is our greatest gift and the most potent thing we have to distribute, because the gospel is Jesus, and Jesus is the good news for which everyone hungers. Irrespective of our program or ministry and regardless of how we meet the needs of the hurting, the hungry, or the hopeless, if we are not offering Jesus, we are not providing anything of eternal value. We must remember this when we think we should flavor our ministries with the latest trends to appeal to the world. Nothing tops Jesus.

The Twelve had to stay connected to Jesus; they had to keep going back because there was not enough in the first baskets they carried to feed the second groups, and the second baskets were insufficient for the third. It is the same for us; we must return to Jesus every day, hour, and minute to have anything to give to anyone. We will run out if we don't stay connected with Jesus, and we will fool ourselves into thinking that giving of ourselves is sufficient. "I didn't have time to go back to Jesus." Seriously? Can you imagine if one of the Twelve had tried that line on that hillside that spring evening? It doesn't work for us, either.

Unfortunately, though, it is not an unusual excuse. Recently, on a Wednesday afternoon, I received an email from a friend who was in a panic, asking if I had any good ideas for teaching children about prayer. Her program's director had forgotten to assign the lesson the previous week, and she was in a bind. It was only hours before the class began, and someone needed to come up with a lesson. There was no time for prayer, no time to come away with Jesus and be ministered to, no time to study, no time to receive what Jesus would have them give the children. I'm sure the children received a lesson that evening, but with what were they fed? And how exhausted was the servant? Did she serve with joy or frustration? How likely is she to continue serving?

Trip after trip, the Twelve carried food to the multitudes, and I wonder, as I try to envision the scene: Did they do it on their own, or did they enlist volunteers to help? Did their dependence on Jesus enable them to ask for help from the crowd? In the Gospel of Marcia (the only basis for my following thoughts), each group saw what was happening. Group Two saw that Group One was eating, and then Group Three saw a full basket heading toward Group Two. In my mind's eye, I don't think that Group Four or Forty just sat there waiting. I believe that people stood up and asked, "How can I help?" because when we see Jesus at work, we want to be a part of it.

Not only do we want to be a part of what Jesus is doing, but as Christians, when we see other believers hard at work bringing God's love to the hurting, the hungry, and the hopeless, we want to help, to share their burdens. No one can carry the load on their own, and it seems that, more often than not, God provides helpers. Paul had Barnabas and Dr. Luke, among many others. King David had Jonathan and then the Thirty Mighty Men. Moses had Aaron. Burdens can be pretty heavy, even burdens of godly service, and I don't think God intended us to bear all the weight by ourselves, but our independence tells us it is good to go alone.

Perhaps it is because of our independence that we struggle with asking for help, because it means we have to admit that we need help. I visited a church once where a youth worker was invited to the front to ask for volunteers for an upcoming event. Her request, as I recall, went something like this: "We are having an event on Saturday morning, and if you find that you don't have anything to do and you happen to think of us and would like to show up, we'd love to have you help. We need some extra hands, but I promise you don't have to teach or do anything that you might think of as work, so if you're bored or find you have some free time on Saturday, we'll be there; you can show up, and we'd appreciate it."

I don't know about you, but that request prompted me to sign up immediately. No, it didn't, and no, I didn't. I'm not sure if anyone did (I have the excuse that I was a visitor, the church was in another country, and I was heading back to the United States on Saturday morning), but what about all the others who sat there and listened to her announcement? Unfortunately, her request for help sounded more like an apology for a potential inconvenience than an invitation to be in the midst of Jesus at work. I hope people showed up to help, even though there wasn't much excitement in the invitation.

Soon after that, when I was at another church, a nursery worker had the microphone and was asking for childcare volunteers for a Thursday morning ministry. She began her call by quoting some things she had heard from the mothers whose children were in her program: "I recently saw my husband commit suicide, and coming here on Thursday mornings is how I keep my eyes on Jesus. I know I will survive this if I hold tight to Jesus." "My husband is deployed, and the love I receive here enables me to be the mom my children need." "I just moved here and don't know anyone; Thursday mornings keep me sane."

Then the nursery worker told the crowd that while Jesus was moving powerfully upstairs in the lives of the moms, if there were no childcare downstairs, the ministry upstairs couldn't happen. She said, "If you want to be a part of what Jesus is doing in these women's lives, then come and show Jesus' love to their children." There were so many volunteers that some had to be turned away. When the light of Jesus shines through us and the work he is doing, we never need to be ashamed to ask people for help. In fact, it is our honor to ask, and it is their privilege to participate.

How do we ask for and secure volunteers? Certainly not by apologizing because we need help. We share what Jesus is doing! Better yet, I suspect many will want to volunteer when they *see* for themselves what Jesus is doing! Can you imagine being on that hillside and *not* wanting to be a part of what was happening? I can't. I would be among the first to raise my hand and ask if I might carry a basket. Why? Because that would get me close enough to see what Jesus was doing. When miracles are happening, I want to see them, don't you? Doesn't everyone?

When others see that Jesus is at work, lives are being changed, and hungry souls are being fed, they will want to participate. Why wouldn't they? Yet, many of us struggle to secure sufficient volunteers for our programs. We have to ask for volunteers all the time, just like they were in the churches I just wrote about. Why? Because sometimes, people don't see Jesus until he is pointed out to them. Only the members of that church who were already a part of the Thursday morning program knew Jesus was at work. The call for volunteers, however, informed everyone!

Another possible reason for a shortage of volunteers is that we don't let Jesus' light shine through us; we block it. Why would we do that? Perhaps it's because we struggle with independence. In our desire to be recognized, we block the light of Jesus with our personal little spotlights, shining them directly onto ourselves, our programs, the weight of our basket, or the size of the crowd. When we do that, we take the credit and the glory, failing to point people to Jesus and what he is doing.

It would have been ridiculous for any of the Twelve to take credit for feeding the people; they were distributors who relied entirely on Jesus to fill their baskets. Another key leadership lesson we need to draw from this event is that we must give Jesus all the credit for what he is doing. The role of the Holy Spirit is to exalt Jesus, and so should we. Jesus taught, *"But when the Helper comes, whom I will send to you from the Father, the Spirit of truth, who proceeds from the Father, he will bear witness about me." "He will glorify me, for he will take what is mine and declare it to you"* (John 15:26; 16:14).

Since the Holy Spirit does not call attention to himself but witnesses to and glorifies Jesus, why do we act as if we can slide Jesus into the background or the shadow of our glory? If our service doesn't promote, celebrate, and exalt Jesus, our service is nothing more than independent self-promotion. Furthermore, once we have elevated ourselves, we think—and then act—as if we are responsible for providing all we could or should have received from Jesus. The result is that we will starve, and so will those we are trying to feed, because we can't conjure up all that is needed to do what God calls us to do. We must back away from anything that puts us in the spotlight. We must discover that our place of ultimate joy is in reflecting the light of Jesus, upon whom and through whom the spotlight of eternity must always shine. All eyes are on Jesus. All glory to Jesus.

Undoubtedly, the Twelve received "thank you's" and heartfelt words of gratitude, just as we do when we serve in God's power for his glory. However, we must never accept these accolades for ourselves. Instead, we should redirect them to the Lord, while humbly accepting every encouragement as if it comes directly from him. We should respond with gratitude for the opportunity to serve in whatever capacity he provides. The Twelve likely never tired of saying, "Did you see, can you see what Jesus is doing? Look up there; get close! Let's go together. I want you to share the joy of distributing all that Jesus is giving!" And that should be our response, too:

"Thank you. God is so gracious to let me serve you. Did you see what he is doing? Can you see it? Come with me; let's go together so you can see all that God is giving."

*To become godly leaders who feed Jesus' sheep with purpose, we **must embrace our role as dependent distributors**, dispensing all that Jesus gives us. We must repent of glory-seeking independence and trust God to fill our baskets. We must rely fully upon God's sufficiency, understanding that our strength and resources come from him.*

Questions for Discussion

1. Who shines brightest in your leadership/service/ministry? What can you learn from them?

2. What has Jesus given you to distribute?

3. Where and to whom do you go when you are empty?

4. Describe when you tried to present an empty basket as full. What was the outcome?

5. How clean are your spiritual hands as you distribute the food Jesus has given you?

6. What filth of the world needs to be washed from your own hands before you serve?

7. How difficult is it for you to ask for volunteers? Why?

8. Have you considered who might step up to work alongside you when they see Jesus at work in and through you?

9. If we are to be billboards for God's grace, what does your billboard proclaim?

Chapter 10
Acknowledge Needs

Bless the Lord, O my soul, and all that is within me, bless his holy name! Bless the Lord, O my soul, and forget not all his benefits, who forgives all your iniquity, who heals all your diseases, who redeems your life from the pit, who crowns you with steadfast love and mercy, who satisfies you with good so that your youth is renewed like the eagle's.
Psalm 103:1–5

We get tired. We get hungry. We over-book and, at times, feel overrun. There is always another hand reaching out for more, another mouth that needs to be fed, another task that needs to be accomplished, and it often seems there are not enough hours in the day to do the things we need to do. We are servants, and we desire to do our work in a godly way, but we are not superhuman. We ask who will meet *our* needs, and then we immediately feel guilty for asking. Yet, we have needs. So did the Twelve.

How much food did Jesus provide that evening? If my previous attempt at math was anywhere near accurate, for each person to receive the equivalent of a fast-food fish sandwich (minus the breading, tartar sauce, and cheese), then each group of about seventy-five people received at least twenty-five pounds of food. If I multiply that by approximately 130 groups (which totals about 9,750 people—a frugal estimate, as some say there were as many as 15,000 people on the hillside that day), that's about 3,250 total pounds of food. Or, and let's not get carried away, say there are 12,000 people; that's 4,000 pounds of bread and fish.

Amazed? I am! And that's assuming each person had only one sandwich. But I suspect an adult woman who isn't dieting or on a date could probably eat a couple of those sandwiches, and an adult man could easily tackle three. And it would be difficult to guess how much a teenage boy would need to feel full. Since everyone ate until satisfied, we are talking about *tons* of food.

Can that be right? Someone check my math, please. How can there be so much at the end when there was so little in the beginning? There is only one answer: Jesus. We must never underestimate Jesus' sufficiency or his ability to satisfy every need, every thirst, and every hunger—including yours and mine as we work to feed his sheep.

While Jesus was feeding thousands that evening, he was also training every person on that hillside, especially the Twelve, that there is never any reason for worry when Jesus is present. And he is always present. Jesus trains them, and us, that we don't need to yield to the temptation to worry about who will meet our needs. We can always trust Jesus' ability to care for us; we will be satisfied as we use everything he provides. *And they all ate and were satisfied* (Mark 6:42). *And when they had eaten their fill, he told his disciples, "Gather up the leftover fragments, that nothing may be lost." So they gathered them up and filled twelve baskets with fragments from the five barley loaves left by those who had eaten* (John 6:12-13).

When Jesus asked Philip, "Where shall we buy bread for these people to eat?" Philip replied, *Two hundred denarii worth of bread would not be enough for each of them to get a little* (John 6:7). "A little." A bite. Philip was thinking small, thinking of the bare minimum necessary to alleviate just enough suffering to get them to the next moment. Jesus wasn't thinking of a little, and Jesus didn't give them a little; he filled their bellies and had twelve baskets of leftovers.

Like the Twelve, we must stop worrying about offering others "just enough" and learn to think bigger. But if we think bigger, won't that require more from us? The fear of exhausting our resources can cause us to hold back, limiting our service to others as we hoard what God has already provided. In truth, we will never have enough unless we are willing to share and use all we have been given. Thinking bigger requires exercising faith that God owns everything and will ensure we have all that we need to serve others as he would. We tend not to reach for the stars because we're afraid we can't grasp them. Faith knows that God created the stars, and they are well within his reach. We often don't look for a miracle because we fear we cannot make the miracle happen. And we can't. But Jesus can.

Jesus' people starve when we, as Christian leaders, worry and hold back, settling for the bare minimum, providing nothing more than a bite, because we are focused on our needs instead of Jesus' sufficiency. Are we content to dispense a morsel when a banquet is possible? Do we set limits on our service because we fear starving as we wonder who will feed us? When we forget all Jesus is capable of doing, we forfeit our front row seats to his miracles.

Worry Is Misplaced Creativity

Knowing they didn't have any food for themselves, the Twelve knew better than to attempt to feed the people. Their initial plan was to send them away, which was not a good strategy because it was born out of fear and shortsightedness, an offspring of worry. An idea conceived by worry and fear births a lousy plan because Jesus is not in it. No one would have eaten anything if the outcome depended on the Twelve. Jesus was the only one with a plan worth appropriating; his design was perfect, and everyone was satisfied. Jesus' perfection always satisfies every need.

Jesus is perfect; he is excellently complete. Jesus, the Second Person of the Trinity, *is the radiance of the glory of God and the exact imprint of his nature* (Hebrews 1:3). *In him the whole fullness of deity dwells bodily* (Colossians 2:9). Jesus is no less God than God the Father is. He is *"Immanuel" (which means God with us)* (Matthew 1:23b). Therefore, all of the attributes of the Triune God dwell within Jesus. He is perfect in wisdom, justice, mercy, grace, beauty, omnipotence, omniscience, will, goodness, love, patience, holiness, peace, wrath, righteousness, and faithfulness.

Though Christ is perfect, we Christians who are *in Christ* are not perfect. God demands righteousness but accepts our belief, crediting it as righteousness; Paul explains this when he teaches about Abraham: *"Abraham believed God, and it was counted to him as righteousness"* (Romans 4:3). The beauty of being in Christ is that God credited Jesus' perfect righteousness to our account by his grace through our faith when we were united with him through his salvific acts. How can this be? We know our hearts, failings, and sins; how can God think of us as righteous without us having earned that righteousness? Grace. Grace is God's unmerited favor poured out on us. God gives us something we desperately need, don't deserve, and cannot earn: right standing with himself.

We cannot achieve or merit a perfect standing before God because we are sinners and cannot clean ourselves enough to stand in his holiness. Therefore, God provided a way for us to be declared righteous—a way to satisfy his holy demand for righteousness. God imputes Christ's righteousness to us when we believe and commit to following Christ. Our sin is exchanged at the cross for Christ's perfect righteousness; *For our sake he made him to be sin who knew no sin, so that in him we might become the righteousness of God* (2 Corinthians 5:21). That is miraculous! Do you want a spectacular salvation story? This is it! The beauty of grace is that it is a gift.

When we believe the gospel: the good news that Jesus, who is God, stepped out of heaven, took on human flesh, and lived a perfect, holy, and righteous life on earth, yet was killed on a criminal's cross, not for his sin (he had no sin), but in our place, as our substitute, and when we appropriate that personally (through faith), then, in the mind of God, we are reckoned as righteous. Christ's perfect righteousness is imputed to us. Though Jesus died, he did not stay dead. Jesus was resurrected to life; he was freed from the agony of death because *it was not possible for him to be held by it* (Acts 2:24). Jesus was raised to life and now sits, exalted, at the right hand of God. His resurrection is not just a historical fact but the hope (the settled assurance) upon which we base our faith. It is the guarantee of our resurrection and eternal life.

Although we have been made perfect in our standing before God, we continue to struggle with our sinful selves. There is a battle raging within us as the Holy Spirit works to make us holy. It's as if the enemy has a stronghold in our hearts and minds, and we are fighting desperately to keep him off the throne of our lives. That enemy is ourselves. We want to sit on our throne and rule over our kingdom. Yet, at the same time, we long to be like Jesus—to be holy as he is holy. We want to live worthy of the great salvation that is ours. And, amazingly, God, in his love, grace, and mercy, has declared that is our destiny: We are *predestined to be conformed to the image of his Son* (Romans 8:29). This is assured because God promises us that *he who begun a good work in you will bring it to completion* (Philippians 1:6). We will be holy.

That is a sweet and precious comfort because sometimes I feel far from holy. The most apparent testimony to my need for continued work toward holiness is that I often fail to trust God's perfection—his perfect provision, timing, wisdom, and sovereignty—over every circumstance of my leadership, service, or ministry, and therefore, I worry. What about you? Do you ever worry about things beyond your control that are perfectly within God's? Do you lie awake at night trying to figure things out or how to make something happen? Do you feel like the Twelve when Jesus said, "You feed them," but there was no food? Worry is proof that we are not trusting God to meet our needs.

We worry when we think God is taking too long or when we think he might not provide all we need, let alone all we want. We worry when the calendar keeps moving, and God doesn't seem to be, and when our numbers slack off or grow too quickly. We worry when we have insufficient leaders to fulfill our ministry slots and when we have too many. We worry about the weather, about budgets, and about buildings. If there is something to be concerned about, we'll worry.

We know that worrying is not trusting, and we know we have a trustworthy God who can satisfy all our needs. Yet we worry. Why? Because we have wonderfully creative imaginations—and worry is misplaced creativity. God is the God of Creation; when he created us, he gave us the ability to imagine great things. But when our great imagination conjures up a myriad of ideas of how God could let us down, fail to provide for us, or not take care of us, we begin to fear, entering a world of sin and error that we created. When we live in worry, we forfeit the satisfaction of seeing God provide, as we worry that whatever he does provide won't be enough.

The worriers on that hillside probably started thinking about breakfast even as they were taking their first bites of dinner. The worriers among the Twelve probably started wondering about where all the people would sleep, even before dinner was finished. The worriers could not fully be in or enjoy the moment because their concerns robbed them of the joy of "now" as they lived in the "what next?" When we are busy worrying, there is no room to celebrate God, because anxiety and celebration can't fit in the same moment—there isn't a moment large enough to hold them both.

Worry tells the world that we don't trust the God we are proclaiming is trustworthy. If we believe his trustworthiness, we wouldn't worry. Therefore, when we choose to worry (and it is a choice), we present an incapable—or unwilling—God. Our worry boldly declares that we fear God cannot—or will not—meet our needs in the best possible way and at the best time. Worry takes over when we look only at our own abilities, pulling us apart emotionally and undermining the pinning of our foundation in God.

What is the antidote to worry? Praise. We cease worrying when we begin praising God and celebrating his character, including his trustworthiness, love, abundance, care, intimacy, and good hand upon our lives. Praise pushes worry right out of the room. There is no place for fear, worry, or anxiety when our hearts are filled with praise. When praise is on our lips, we stop worrying, sit quietly before the Lord, and wait patiently for him. *Trust in the Lord and do good; dwell in the land and befriend faithfulness. Delight yourself in the Lord, and he will give you the desires of your heart. Commit your way to the Lord; trust in him and he will act. He will bring forth your righteousness as the light, and your justice as the noonday. Be still before the Lord and wait patiently for him; fret not yourself* (Psalm 37:3–7a).

Jesus trained the Twelve to trust him; nevertheless, they didn't always get every lesson right the first time. And let's not forget that they even missed Jesus' teaching about the resurrection. After the crucifixion, they thought Jesus was dead and didn't anticipate a resurrection until they saw the empty tomb; some believed only when Jesus appeared in their midst. And truth be told, if they could miss something that big, that's a comfort to me. I know that I won't always get everything right, but although God is gracious and forgiving, that doesn't mean I am off the hook, and neither are you. We must continue to strive to trust Jesus completely. He is perfect, and his plans are perfect. He will accomplish his plans in his perfect time, and when he does, you and I will be satisfied. Worry keeps me from getting things right. Trusting Jesus leads me to contentment, satisfaction, and peace.

There Is Always Enough Where Jesus Is at Work

As we trust Jesus to meet our needs, there may be times he goes beyond everything we could ever imagine, just as he did with the Twelve: there were leftovers! As I think about it, in every ministry I've ever served in, when we faithfully prayed, trusted in, and relied entirely upon Jesus, not only were those we served spiritually fed, but there was often plenty left over for those of us who were serving. The great thing about being a servant to God's people is that he uses us to lead and meet the needs of others, and he uses them to meet our needs. Everybody eats.

There was a time in my life when I was spiritually starving. We landed in Missouri after having moved around the Midwest multiple times over a handful of years, during which we were never in one place long enough to put our roots down deep in any church. Desperate to connect and make friends, I looked up a Bible study I had attended in another state years before. I contacted the leadership of the class, and sure enough, because I had previously held leadership positions, I was invited to interview for a leadership position there.

Over coffee, I told the head of the class that I would do anything. As I recall, my exact words were, "I will even wash toilets, if that's where you need me." I was so worried they might not have a place for me that I made a rash promise. I did say I was desperate to connect, didn't I? There was nothing to worry about; there was a place of service for me. But, horror of horrors, she asked me to serve in the children's program. With 3-year-olds. Twenty-one of them. I am embarrassed to tell you the first two thoughts that blitzed through my mind like bolts of lightning were, first: Well, that's a waste of talent (OK, I had a little pride issue God needed to work on); and second: I don't like little children (OK, I adored my own two precious angels, but other than that, I had a bit of a love issue God needed to work on).

Working with children was not exactly my dream job, but truth be told, neither was washing toilets. Thank heaven she didn't ask me to do that! So, with a self-righteous smile plastered on my face, I replied, "Of course, I'll serve wherever God would have me." She graciously smiled and assured me she would pray for me, as would the children's program supervisor (hmm, did she see me as Jesus saw me?). She had no idea how much prayer I needed. I was stepping out of my comfort zone for selfish reasons and had no idea how to serve little children. Lots of little children. I had no training. I had no resources. And worst of all, I didn't have sufficient love for them.

They prayed. And I walked into the classroom. It was as I expected: every orifice on every face of every child that could leak was leaking. There were runny noses, drooling mouths, and teary eyes in abundance—this was well before hand sanitizer dispensers were mounted by every door. My pocket pack of tissues was quickly depleted. This was not what I wanted nor what I thought I needed. Nevertheless, I had committed to serve, so I stepped in with both feet and a quick prayer. Then, miraculously, within just a few minutes, God somehow instantly changed my heart. That day, and every week after, as I'd sit in the circle with those precious little ones who were hungering and thirsting for God, I learned how to tell a Bible story, not just recite one, but tell it with passion. I fell in love with twenty-one 3-year-olds, and I fell in love with the Word of God in a whole new way. I felt like a momma bird feeding her hungry babies the delicious bread of life. I could hardly wait to be with my little ones week after week, to hug them, love them, and share God and his Word with them. As I served the children,

God used them to train and serve me. He was meeting a need I didn't know I had.

Little did I know that in just a few years, God would call me to lead the class and teach the women. I'll never forget the first time I stood in the pulpit and looked out at a sanctuary filled with spiritually hungry women; I saw the same anticipation on their faces as I had seen on those little 3-year-olds. The only difference was that my new nest was a little bigger, yet it was still filled with God's children who desired to be fed by the Word of God. There was never a reason to worry; God always had a place for me and heart-filling satisfaction in that place.

God perfectly met my need to feel connected to that new community. He also met my need to serve his people and used my service to train me for future service. God has a fantastic way of weaving together all of his purposes through the lives of his children. *For as in one body we have many members, and the members do not all have the same function, so we, though many, are one body in Christ, and individually members one of another. Having gifts that differ according to the grace given to us, let us use them: if prophecy, in proportion to our faith; if service, in our serving; the one who teaches, in his teaching; the one who exhorts, in his exhortation; the one who contributes, in generosity; the one who leads, with zeal; the one who does acts of mercy, with cheerfulness* (Romans 12:4-8).

When we each do precisely what God would have us do without worrying about what God is doing, we will meet the needs of others, and God will meet our needs. When we worry, we tend to scrimp and conserve, cutting corners and holding back. However, there is no room for frugality when we trust God because God is not frugal. God tells us that we must serve with lavish generosity, for we will reap the same way we sow. We can be generous when we trust God to meet every need. *The point is this: whoever sows sparingly will also reap sparingly, and whoever sows bountifully will also reap bountifully...And God is able to make all grace abound to you, so that having all sufficiency in all things at all times, you may abound in every good work. As it is written, "He has distributed freely, he has given to the poor; his righteousness endures forever." He who supplies seed to the sower and bread for food will supply and multiply your seed for sowing and increase the harvest of your righteousness. You will be enriched in every way to be generous in every way, which through us will produce thanksgiving to God* (2 Corinthians 9:6, 8-11).

We must not worry that there won't be enough for us. It stands to reason that the more we serve, the more we are served; the more we are joyful in our service, the more we will be able to rejoice; we cannot out-give God. When we first seek to honor him, exalt the name of Jesus, and serve for his glory, God will meet our needs. There is no room for worry. Worry prompts us to hoard our lives and resources, striving to meet our own needs and serving only ourselves, fearful that since there might not be enough for us, we surely can't give out more than we have. Worry places God low on our list of priorities, and why should God be generous with us if he is not first in our lives?

The Israelites learned this lesson after the Babylonian exile. Once the remnant had returned to Jerusalem, they delayed rebuilding the temple while building their own paneled houses. Did they worry that God would not provide homes for them? The prophet Haggai spoke for the Lord and said, "*Consider your ways. You have sown much, and harvested little. You eat, but you never have enough; you drink, but you never have your fill. You clothe yourselves, but no one is warm. And he who earns wages does so to put them in a bag with holes.*" "*You looked for much, and behold, it came to little. And when you brought it home, I blew it away. Why? declares the Lord of hosts. Because of my house that lies in ruins, while each of you busies himself with his own house*" (Haggai 1:5-6, 9).

God must have priority in our lives and our service. We will lack nothing when we commit to him, and the outflow of our love for him is obedience. In obedience, as we put God first, we honor him. We trust him. We give him allegiance. And he promises he will never let us down. *"Bring the full tithe into the storehouse, that there may be food in my house. And thereby put me to the test, says the Lord of hosts, if I will not open the windows of heaven for you and pour down for you a blessing until there is no more need"* (Malachi 3:10).

We must not worry about out-giving God in any arena, even as the Scripture above states, financially. But our treasures are more than financial. What about time? Love? Service? Commitment? We are like the Twelve; our baskets are empty unless God fills them, and we cannot be stingy once he does. We can't hold on to anything and expect it to be multiplied.

Scrimping out of fear or worry is, in reality, pride. It is thinking that I am more important or worthy of my resources than anyone else is. Fearing that there won't be enough for others occurs when we rely only on ourselves to refill the coffers, shelves, or pantry sufficiently. Our stinginess doesn't trust God. As we pour out our lives and hearts to serve God's people, God will meet our needs, and it shouldn't surprise us if there are leftovers.

There is perfection in every act of God. He knows our needs, and he meets them as we trust him. Why would we not trust him? The transcendent God—who created and ordered the universe, keeps the earth from falling, the sun from burning out, and the moon from crashing down—cares about the smallest detail of our lives. Though we may seem like no more than one of the billions of dust specks in a ray of sunshine, God knows us individually and cares about us. God lives outside of his creation and is independent of it, yet he is also immanent: dwelling within his creation. And his creation is wholly and utterly dependent upon him. Our dependence on him reveals our trust in him. He will meet our needs.

When we think of God's unending, overwhelming, magnificent, lavish love for us, which he proved on the cross, it is unthinkable not to trust him. We need not worry about today or tomorrow, money, volunteers, schedules, or any other detail. Seriously, is anything too much for God to handle? Is anything more valuable to God than you and the work he has called you to do? Do you seriously think that God will not be involved in every detail?

He loves us and knows every detail of our lives. We can trust that he will provide for us. We must not let our fears or worries stop us from serving wherever he calls us. The same God who fed more than five thousand hungry souls with a little bit of bread and a couple of fish has called you to serve him. Do you seriously think he'll let you down? Do you think he won't give you whatever you need if you ask for it? Our leadership did not start with us; it began with God. It will not end with our inability; it will succeed with God's ability.

As we've worked through this miracle, sometimes I wonder at what point the Twelve did take time to eat. As they were serving? After everyone else was served? Did they eat first? We don't know. We know who fed them, what they ate, that they were satisfied, and that there were leftovers for the next day. Jesus met every need and attended to every detail, even the available baskets. How else would they carry food to the people and hold all the leftovers? God meets every need. Every single one. Every single time. And always with satisfaction.

We may have to forfeit sleep, we may have to wait to eat, we may have to carry heavy loads, and we may have to ask for volunteers to help us bear our burdens, but we will never have to do anything without God. There are limitations to what we can do, and it is wise to know them, but our limitations must never be used as an excuse to limit God or to indulge in fear. No one thought five thousand men, plus women, children, and twelve disciples, would eat that day. The limitations of the Twelve were evident, and their needs were many, yet everyone ate until they were satisfied and had leftovers. There was no need for worry.

*To become godly leaders who feed Jesus' sheep with steadfastness **we must acknowledge that we are needy**. However, we must repent of worrying about ourselves and our needs. As we trust God to provide, we will overcome worry, live generously, and find our satisfaction in Jesus.*

Questions for Discussion

1. Do your fears limit God?

2. Do your worries keep you from serving God?

3. What is your primary concern in your service? Seeking God's glory and honor, or meeting the needs of your ministry/service/leadership?

4. In what area are you waiting on God? To combat worry as you wait, which attribute of God might you praise?

5. How is God meeting your needs today?

6. What worry do you need to lay at his feet and rest as you wait?

7. What was the last worry that woke you up in the middle of the night and kept you awake?

8. What miracle are you asking God for?

9. In what area of your leadership are you settling for a bite when God might have a banquet ready?

10. What specific tools do you use to overcome worry in the areas of your greatest need?

Chapter 11

Surrender

*On his robe and on his thigh he has this
name written, King of kings and Lord of lords.
Revelation 19:16*

As servants in the kingdom of God, we serve purposefully. We have goals and work for change—to change things and people and circumstances. We want success—for our plans to succeed and to bear much fruit. But what if our service is about something other than what we can change? What if it is about how *we* are to change? Jesus told us, *"Truly, truly, I say to you, unless a grain of wheat falls into the earth and dies, it remains alone; but if it dies, it bears much fruit"* (John 12:24). Maybe our service is about learning to die so that we can help others to live. What if we must die to our desires, programs, and agendas so that we can accurately help the people we serve find abundant life?

Jesus fed the multitude, and the lives of thousands of people would never be the same after that meal. To say they were a part of something spectacular is an understatement. They were fed from the hand of God, their bellies were fully satisfied, and I think we can safely say that they didn't want it to end. In a culture where the bare necessities of food, shelter, and clothing consumed one's daily routine, this miraculous meal had to have been revolutionary. They received unlimited food and considered Jesus their key to a life of ease and comfort. It was as if they had won the lottery. They wanted to crown him as their king and let him feed them forever.

Wouldn't you? Wouldn't I? Come to think of it, isn't that how many people want Christianity to be? Let's sign on with Jesus and have a life of ease. And isn't that the way some people present the gospel? Name it and claim it! Jesus wants you to have it all! Jesus will protect you from all harm! There's power available; tap into it! Let go, and let God! Get out of the way and let God take over—no more struggle. Stand still, and he will fight your battles for you. All this, and heaven, too! Who's in? It would be difficult to decline. But is that the way it is?

Jesus taught the disciples, the multitudes, and now you and me that being a Christian is not a life of gimme, gimme, gimme, but a life of surrender, sacrifice, and suffering. As servants, we must learn and understand that following Jesus means letting go of self: self-promotion, self-focus, self-satisfaction, self-reliance, self-whatever; it is dying to self and living for Jesus. It is a life of self-denial, of losing one's life to gain it. It is a life that requires letting go. *When the people saw the sign that he had done, they said, "This is indeed the Prophet who is to come into the world!" Perceiving then that they were about to come and take him by force to make him king, Jesus withdrew again to the mountain by himself* (John 6:14-15). *Immediately he made his disciples get into the boat and go before him to the other side, to Bethsaida, while he dismissed the crowd* (Mark 6:45).

Jesus knew the crowd intended to make him king. Moreover, he also knew how persuadable the Twelve were at that moment. What conversations did each group have? As they received the first baskets of food, were they filled with gratitude, honor, and praise? Did self-focus prompt them to imagine how their lives would be if Jesus kept this up for them and only them? Did the loudest voice muster up a consensus? Were the groups persuaded, one at a time, to join the others, as they banded together to make Jesus their leader? There must have been influential voices and strong personalities in that crowd. How easy it would have been to capture the hearts of the Twelve and convince them to join the mob and crown Jesus as their king.

Wasn't that what the Twelve wanted anyway? Wasn't that a big part of why they were with him? Didn't they jockey over who would sit in the seats of honor at his right and left when he came into his kingdom? Was this the time? Was this the moment? Was this the coronation? The crowd thought so, but Jesus knew it was not the time nor the place, nor was this the crowd that would see him crowned the King of kings and the Lord of lords.

Jesus was in control. He always has been. He always will be. The Twelve needed to learn that nothing can thwart God's plans: not them, a crowd, nor a majority agreement. No power in the universe outside of God—and indeed not any popularity vote—can change God's purpose and always-perfect timing. We all must learn this lesson repeatedly, day by day and moment by moment. It does not behoove us to promote our program, agenda, ideas, or schedule above God's. Jesus was training them to see him as he is, to let him be who he is, and to stop trying to force him to fit into their mold. They could do that only as they surrendered their desires, service, and lives to him.

Godly Leaders Surrender Our Desires

The multitude received the food, but they missed the point. Jesus performed this miracle, this sign, to show them who he was, not merely what he could do. When Jesus multiplied the bread and the fish, he revealed his authority over nature, physics, and creation. He brought to light that he is God, the One who could save and sustain them for all eternity, not just feed them for a day. The crowd wanted daily bread more than the Bread of Life. They missed the truth on that hillside, and they missed it the next day when they went searching for more free food.

When they found Jesus and asked for bread, rather than feed their bodies, Jesus offered to feed their souls. *Jesus said to them, "I am the bread of life; whoever comes to me shall not hunger, and whoever believes in me shall never thirst… This is the bread that comes down from heaven, so that one may eat of it and not die. I am the living bread that came down from heaven. If anyone eats of this bread, he will live forever. And the bread that I will give for the life of the world is my flesh" (John 6:35, 50-51).*

That was not what the people wanted; they desired something else. They wanted what Jesus could give, not who Jesus was. They began to grumble and complain. Jesus wasn't doing what they expected, and when they were brought to a place of decision, they chose to leave Jesus. The thrill-seekers weren't the only ones who rejected Jesus; *After this many of his disciples turned back and no longer walked with him* (John 6:66). They deserted him.

Their level of fickleness astounds me; only hours before, Jesus had miraculously fed them, and now, the next day, his teaching was too strong, so they left. No, I guess I'm not astounded; I'm more convicted. Am I, are you, too often like this crowd?

The Bible has much to say about many things; some words are sweet and easy to digest, while some are tough to chew. When we encounter challenging passages, we have to meditate on them, read commentaries, research meanings of words, find the cultural context, and dig deep to understand what God is saying to us. And when we do, we have a choice: Do we accept hard truths, or do we walk away?

I conversed with a friend about a specific biblical doctrine the other day—one that he dismissed, but which the Christian faith is founded upon. When I countered his argument with Scripture, my friend replied, "No, I don't believe that. The Bible is wrong there." Is the Bible wrong? He walked away when the Word of God was not what he wanted to hear.

We may twist words or ignore entire passages to force the Bible to say what we want, but that doesn't change what it says. We must let God speak for himself. Attempting to manipulate him or his words is futile. The truth will always prevail.

As we serve wholeheartedly in the place where Jesus has called us, and when we believe we know what Jesus should do in a given situation, do we force the circumstances to align with our ideas? Or do we move gingerly as we continually seek God's guidance and remain flexible should God change our path at any given moment? We expect God to bless our inclination and move us forward. But when the confirmation doesn't come, is it not beyond us to pout, walk away, or walk full speed ahead without God? When God doesn't give us what we want or what we expect, do we still want him?

It is not pretty, but it happens. We may not walk away from Jesus and our salvation, but we are not above walking away from what he would have us do. There was once a woman who served alongside me who consistently took trips that prevented her from attending the scheduled weekly training sessions. It had been clearly explained to us that we couldn't lead the following week if we did not participate in the training. Why? Because our personal spiritual growth is more important than our leadership availability. Attending the sessions was where we, as leaders, had our baskets filled, were ministered to, and were equipped to give out what Jesus gave us. This person decided that too much was asked of her. She turned away.

I had another acquaintance who moved to a community far from where we attended church. After much prayer, she felt God's call to go to a church nearer her new home, where she could invite her neighbors, participate in mid-week events, and serve more frequently. She was excited about moving to this new church and all the opportunities the transition would afford. However, when she asked if a leadership position was available, she was told there were none, though they welcomed her warmly to worship with them. But she wanted to be a leader. She decided that obeying God's call to move to a new church home without an immediate place of leadership was too harsh. She turned away.

Do we desire what we want from Jesus more than we long to follow and serve him? When push comes to shove, do we only want to serve ourselves? If we sincerely yearn to feed Jesus' sheep, we must be sincerely intent on following Jesus wherever he leads. Loving Jesus as he is, not as we think he should be, is vital to our Christian leadership. We follow Jesus because we love him. Period.

Godly Leaders Surrender Our Service

If we want to feed God's people without starving ourselves, we must remember that it is not *what* we can do for or give others, but *who* we can give them. We must give them Jesus. We must present him in all of his beautiful majesty. We must serve out of obedient love and point those we serve to Jesus through our words and actions, including submission to him as he is and as he calls us to be. Our service must be surrendered to Jesus.

As we submit our service to Jesus, we become channels of his love, grace, and mercy. When people experience Jesus through us, *he* is what they will want—not our program, our ministry, or even ourselves—even though it may be *through* our program, our ministry, or ourselves that others may find him. The focus of our service must always be on bringing Jesus, not the bread or the fish, the disciples, the program, or the life-skills classes. Our main mission is not to offer sermons, lectures, childcare, materials, crafts, or songs. While programs and ministries are important, they are merely tools, nothing more than the baskets through which we can bring Jesus to those who need him. We are the sacred go-betweens, given the privilege of bringing Jesus to hungry souls.

Thousands on the hillside—many whom Jesus healed and prayed over, who witnessed miracles and ate until they were satisfied—missed the point. How much more likely is it that those we serve will miss the point if we do not make a concerted effort to point them to Jesus? There is always a shiny thing to distract us. It is too easy for our programs, ministries, events, giveaways, music, and leadership personalities to distract from Jesus. Anything—a formula, an idea, a popularity contest, a reputation, even the day of the week we meet together—can become a distraction.

The fish sandwich was the shiny thing for the thousands on the hillside. That sandwich distracted them from who Jesus was. It was what they needed, but its fulfillment was temporary. Whatever we offer besides Jesus is temporary. The temporary food they received drew their attention away from the eternal food that Jesus was offering. If we let anything other than Jesus be the focal point, how can we expect those we serve to desire Jesus? We can't. Everyone's eyes follow the spotlight, and if we allow our program, agenda, service, or even personality to outshine our presentation of Jesus, the thing that wins them will become their focus. Whatever avenue God has given us to serve or lead, we must be vigilant that our focus is always on Jesus. We must not turn the spotlight on whatever shiny thing we may be using to bring them Jesus.

If God has called us to servant leadership in a program, we must not promote the program over Jesus. If we do, then the loyalty of those we serve will be to the program; that is what they will promote. It is possible to win converts to how we study the Bible, minister to the needy, feed the homeless, or do church, and not win them to Jesus. When that happens, we merely convert them to our way of thinking, working, or serving. If we do not promote the gospel, any conversion is a mental assent to what we do or say; there is no heart change, rebirth, or commitment to Christ.

When the program or personality fails or ends (and they all eventually do), those won to anything other than Jesus will fall away because there will be nothing left to hold them secure. Do you know people who have walked away from their profession of faith because a pastor moved, a church closed, or a program ended? Only as Jesus is the heart of a program and the reason for the program, and only as long as the program exists to serve his people for his glory, will the recipients see Jesus and choose him. Only then will they want to make him the rightful King over their lives. Only then will God continue to bless the program. When we veer from this goal, beware; God's blessing could very well be lifted.

We must be vigilant in our leadership so as not to serve with an underlying ideological plan. We must come without an agenda and regularly examine our hearts to verify that we are not promoting an agenda over Jesus. We should double-check the spotlight's angle daily to ensure it is not pointing at ourselves or our agenda but always upon Jesus, who defines us and establishes our goals. Just like the Twelve who were about to succumb to the mob mentality of the crowd, we can become so convinced that our agenda and what we want to accomplish are of utmost importance that we fall into patterns of self-serving leadership without even knowing it.

It is of vital importance that we have godly friends and church leaders who hold us accountable. Insisting that the way we think, interpret the Bible, or believe and practice that belief is the only right way for Christians is a red flag indicating that we have crossed a line—the spotlight has shifted away from Jesus and onto ourselves. And when those in authority over us or who walk in love beside us speak up, it would do us well to listen and heed their words of rebuke.

When we promote our programs, agendas, or ourselves over Jesus, we are not serving in a way that brings hope and respite; instead, we are providing little more than a diversion. Our service does not help anyone; it simply keeps us and those we desire to serve busy. When we are busy, we don't focus on Jesus as the answer to our needs; Jesus becomes an afterthought, and the gospel is lost. Heaven forbid we think we are a success when our programs or agenda prevail and Jesus is missed. Jesus is the only hope for hurting and lost people. He must be the food we bring, the goal of our programs, and the substance of our agendas.

Any service or leadership not marked by submission is prideful. It is a leadership of control that promotes our agenda to keep us in control. The only person who is genuinely served when we promote ourselves is ourselves—this cannot be the goal of the godly leader. A godly leader selflessly serves Jesus and others, allowing Jesus to set the agenda. A godly leader gives Jesus room to work in the lives of those they serve. Godly servants step out of the spotlight and let the Holy Spirit within them promote and exalt Jesus through them.

How easy it would have been for any of the Twelve to say, "Look at me bringing this food!" How foolish it would have sounded. Yet we say things like: "Do you see me serving? Leading? Ministering to these people?" We may not say those things out loud, but we think them, and if not in those words, in similar ones. If the motive of our service is to serve ourselves, then to what are we converting the people we serve? Is it to us? Is it to a works religion? Do our converts feel they must be as busy as we are to be as holy as we are?

To serve with a motive that is anything other than serving Jesus is fruitless. We don't serve for fanfare; no one needs to know what we are doing. We don't have to be at church every time the doors open. We are not the only capable ones. Our motto must not be, "Who will if I don't?" If we do what we have been equipped to do and give others the space to do what they've been equipped to do, everything will get done, and Jesus will receive the glory.

What is your motive for leadership? Do you stay busy to keep from feeling worthless? Do you serve as an attempt to earn God's favor? We would all like to say that our primary motive for service to Jesus is because we love him, but is it always? If, in all things, we took to heart the words of God—*Whatever you do, work heartily, as for the Lord and not for men* (Colossians 3:23)—then our motives would be honorable, biblical, and good. However, when our service is more about ourselves and what we get out of it—notoriety, self-fulfillment, or praise—we are serving ourselves, not Jesus. If we've forgotten whom we serve, it is time to do a heart-check: Ask Jesus to search your heart for any offensive thing, then confess, repent, and dedicate your surrendered service to him.

Godly Leaders Surrender Our Lives

Jesus must always be the reason for our service. When he is King of our lives—when we recognize that he is the One who loves us the most and we respond to him in love—others will see that he is a worthy King. He will then be the King others want to serve. God gives us all gifts to use for the edification of the church, and some of us are servants at heart—we enjoy helping others and taking a less visible role. However, as we stated at the beginning of this book, servants lead, and leaders serve; and people want to follow strong leaders. A spirit of leadership attracts people. Even if you don't think of yourself as charming, outgoing, or worthy of attention, if you have the gift of leadership, the people you serve will follow you. Who doesn't appreciate the one who cares for them, helps meet their needs, and humbly serves them?

Unfortunately, we sometimes put godly servants on pedestals they don't ask for or deserve. When we place our pastors, teachers, elders, deacons, deaconesses, and many other leaders on pedestals, we are disappointed when they fall. If you are a leader, chances are, someone has placed you on one. If you are new to leadership, you can expect it eventually. Heaven forbid we begin to enjoy the view from the pedestal. When that happens, the natural bent is to pull away from Jesus and work independently of his authority as we try to maintain our balance. When we do, since we have no authority apart from God's, our perch grows even more wobbly. God will brook no rivals, and pedestals, especially public ones, will all fail. It is not fun to fall, but fall, we will.

As we humbly serve, we will use our personality, life experiences, heartaches, sorrows, dark times, and joys as illustrations to help others see how the Almighty has ministered to us. Every experience God has given us becomes a touch point in serving others. Still, the light of our personal experiences should never outshine Jesus, the Light of the World. We may be salt and light, but we are not The Light; we are reflections of his True Light, and we must constantly point people to him.

I am reminded of a tragic story that illustrates the heartbreak of a woman who grew up in the Christian church, professed her faith in Jesus, and was baptized as a teen. As a young adult, she got married and raised her family to attend church, but by midlife, she left the church and decided she was an agnostic. When asked why, she said she had "tried that whole born-again thing once, but it didn't work for me." How can being born again not work? One is either born again or not; it is not a role to try on or take off.

I've pondered that story often, and when I do, I invariably land on two questions: First, what was the basis for her profession of faith? Someone's agenda? A roll call? Empty facts? A promise of a life of ease? A guarantee of overcoming power? A formula? A winning personality? And, second, in what had she placed the faith she professed: An argument that she couldn't refute or master? A church membership list? A bed of ease that couldn't sustain a life of suffering? A promise of overcoming power that failed her as she yielded to temptations? A formula that produced nothing of value? A personality that moved on? Empty words?

Does this story break your heart? This lost soul professed faith in Jesus, yet she didn't know him. She was baptized, but into what? Her faith was placed in whatever she heard that sounded good and won her heart. Was she told about the sin that separates us from God and the promise of reconciliation through the blood of Jesus? Had anyone taught her about grace and why it is so amazing? It seems that she was not won to the gospel of Jesus. If she had been won to Jesus, she would have received him and been born again by the Holy Spirit. Regeneration, being *"born of water and the Spirit"* (John 3:5), cannot be undone any more than one can undo one's physical birth. I wonder if this is why we see an increase in once-professing Christians now proclaiming a deconstructed faith; they never were truly born again.

We cannot save anyone. We cannot change anyone. We can only bring them Jesus. And, when we bring Jesus through our service—alongside whatever else we offer to meet whatever temporary needs—when we highlight, praise, and give Jesus the glory, people will come to a place of decision: Do I choose this Jesus as my King? My Sovereign? My Lord? Everyone will one day have to decide who Jesus is and whether they will commit to him or walk away. Shouldn't that be the aim and motive for every act of godly service: to bring Jesus to people so they can see him and decide for themselves who Jesus is? Do the people you serve see Jesus?

On that hillside, all eyes were on Jesus, and everyone there, including the Twelve, wanted to make him king. It wasn't the right time, the right way, or the right place. Jesus' timing, wisdom, and knowledge are perfect; he knew their motives and did not submit to their attempt to make him into something he was not. He does not submit to us either.

Just as the Twelve had to learn to submit to Jesus, so must we. We cannot manipulate Jesus' timing or purpose any more than they could. We cannot expect to push Jesus into our mold and force him to perform for us in the manner we dictate, any more than they could. Jesus is God; as God, he has every right to dictate what we must do, not vice versa.

Only as we see and accept the reality of Jesus, that he is indeed King of kings and Lord of lords, and embrace the truth that we are here to serve him selflessly, not the other way around, do we take on the same mindset as John the Baptist, who said, *"He must increase, but I must decrease"* (John 3:30). The basis for our surrendered lives, service, and desires is not to earn Jesus' favor, or to appear more spiritual; it is that we love him, the One who first loved us. In the same proportion that Jesus prevails in our hearts, he is preeminent in our service. Only as his Spirit fills us can we keep the spotlight of glory squarely on Jesus and serve fully surrendered to him.

To become godly leaders who feed Jesus' sheep with truth and joy, we must **surrender to Jesus as our King**. *We must repent of any motive besides love for him and his children. As Jesus becomes more, we will become less and overcome every obstacle preventing surrender.*

Questions for Discussion

1. Do you follow the crowd when thinking about Jesus? Or do you follow Jesus?

2. Describe a time when you deliberately chose to die to yourself to be of service to Jesus.

3. Where are you settling for what Jesus can give rather than for who he is?

4. Do you find yourself promoting your program at times when you should be promoting Jesus?

5. When is it most challenging to set aside your agenda?

6. Does busyness describe your service?

7. What tempts you to independence?

8. What is most difficult for you: Surrendering your wants, service, or life?

9. Have you ever put anyone on a spiritual pedestal? What was the result?

10. Have you been placed on a pedestal? Are you on one now? Does that concern you? What will you do about it?

11. What is your plan to give God the glory for your service?

CHAPTER 12

It Is Impossible to Expend the Eternal

*"Lord, you know everything; you know that I love you."
Jesus said to him, "Feed my sheep."*
John 21:17b

Feed my sheep. Jesus tells us to do it, just as he told Peter. And he will see to it that we can do it, just as he did for the Twelve. We've looked at ten timeless truths for godly service that help us rely on Jesus and accomplish the service he has prepared for us. We know that only as his Spirit fills us can we serve without tiring out, feed his sheep without starving, and reflect his glory ongoingly. When we submit to Jesus, his bright and eternal light shines through us. As we decrease and he increases, people see Jesus and will want to make him the King of their lives. It wasn't the right time for the multitude on the hillside, but it is the right time now.

After the thousands who followed Jesus ate their fill of food, they sought him again the next day, and then they just as quickly abandoned him when they discovered that he would not bend to fit their expectations. When Jesus told them that the cost of following him included appropriating him—taking him into their being and letting him be their lives—they decided the price was too high, and most of them left. But not everyone. *When many of his disciples heard it, they said, "This is a hard saying; who can listen to it?"... After this many of his disciples turned back and no longer walked with him. So Jesus said to the twelve, "Do you want to go away as well?" Simon Peter answered him, "Lord, to whom shall we go? You have the words of eternal life, and we have believed, and have come to know that you are the Holy One of God"* (John 6:60, 66–69).

To whom shall we go? This same question is asked of you and me. To serve God's people, we must go to Jesus and lead others to him. Only Jesus can meet their needs; only Jesus can meet ours. The thousands who ate the bread on that hillside thought they'd never again have to plant the grain in the hot sun, till the soil, sit at the mercy of God waiting for timely rain, and figure out how to persevere through drought or flood. Never again would they have to harvest the wheat, winnow the chaff, haul the grain bags to the mill, and grind it into flour. There would be no more back-bending labor—kneading dough, chopping and carrying firewood, and stoking ovens as they burned their fingers. Never again would they have to fish day and night on an untrustworthy sea. There would be no more nets to mend in the hot sun. And the days of looking into hungry faces, explaining why there was no food, would end. Thousands missed the promise of eternal life because they were focused on gaining an easier life.

Are things different today? There are programs and servants galore, yet people are feeding on substitutes: promises of comfort and hopes for lives of ease. We deprive them of abundant life when we don't offer the Bread of Life. People won't naturally see Jesus in our service just as they didn't see him on that hillside; they saw food. We must be intentional about bringing and revealing Jesus. We must tell people why we do what we do, and our actions must align with our words. If we humbly practice the timeless principles outlined in this book, everyone will see that we serve Jesus, and it is only because of that that we serve others well.

If we are going to be godly leaders, servants who never grow tired of serving, and leaders who lead others to Jesus, we must focus our eyes on who Jesus truly is: He is life. We must work to bring that life to those we are serving. We have the most incredible privilege to introduce those we serve to Jesus, who prayed to God for us, saying, *"And this is eternal life: that they know you, the only true God, and Jesus Christ whom you have sent"* (John 17:3).

If our goal as leaders is to serve Jesus' sheep, we must first know what they ultimately need: Jesus. Only by giving themselves to Christ Jesus will they experience eternal life. If we tend to physical needs without ministering to spiritual needs, we are not offering the Bread of Life; we are merely offering the same bread available from any secular program. That bread will eventually be gone. Only eternal life will remain.

The principles of leadership that we've looked at were true over two thousand years ago, and they are true today. To be godly leaders who efficiently and effectively feed Jesus' sheep without starving to death, we will appropriate Jesus—take him into our lives and let him direct us as Lord—because we can only lead as Jesus taught the disciples to lead. It is only as we are connected to Jesus and living in him that we can:

- Start with Jesus—his call, his salvation, his strength.
- Work with Jesus to hone our vision.
- Embrace the tests that mature our faith.
- Believe that nothing is too difficult for God.
- Know that what God requires, God provides.
- Let go of the chaos and embrace God's order.
- Pray continually with gratitude in all circumstances.
- Embrace our role as dependent distributors.
- Acknowledge that God meets our needs.
- Lead in surrender.

It is easier to aspire to these principles than to practice them. We are fallen humans who continually fight against our sinful nature as it rears up and tempts us to find a shortcut, take control "just this once," or doubt whether God is all he says he is and will do all that he says he will do. However, as we learn in the book of James, the way to overcome any and every temptation is to remember how good God is and that *Every good gift and every perfect gift is from above, coming down from the Father of lights, with whom there is no variation of shadow due to change* (James 1:17). God is the giver of all good things. He will not withhold that which is good from his children; therefore, we do not have to follow the dictates of our sinful nature, focusing on what we don't have or complaining because what we do have isn't what we want. We have the power of the Holy Spirit within us to put to death the misdeeds of our desires. We can choose to live and lead in the Spirit.

By remembering that it is impossible to expend the eternal, and as we allow the Spirit to control us, we will not tire of doing good. We should be energized by the truth that we cannot use up or consume completely what is eternal because the eternal is infinite. Jesus is the eternal God; as long as we have life and breath and dwell in Christ Jesus, we have everything we need to give all God asks of us. In Christ, and only in Christ, we can become the godly leaders he has called us to be, equipped to sufficiently feed his sheep without fear of going hungry.

Jesus took time to show the Twelve and us to how to overcome our hesitancies, fears, previous failures, inadequacies, and especially our busyness by spending time with him. He calls us to rest in him and allow him to serve us before we begin to serve others. He teaches us to overcome our shortsightedness and see others with compassion, as he sees them. He encourages us to set aside our self-reliance, trusting in his sufficiency as he involves us precisely where he has planned our service. He teaches us to abandon our pride and submit to his authority as we rely entirely on him to equip us. He enables us to overcome chaos and embrace godly order in every aspect of our lives. He challenges us to live in gratitude, grow in our contentment, and step out of the spotlight, letting go of our self-serving thinking and self-promoting ways, and shining gloriously—for him and in him.

Jesus calls us to obey him; he is wise, loving, and longs for the best for us, so our obedience to him yields abundant blessings. He teaches us to be generous and give without fear of giving out. He guides us to pray for what we have and don't have, and commands us to be grateful in everything, teaching us that his will for us is good. He offers us the opportunity to serve the ones he has placed in front of us, humbly seeking his help. He teaches us to trust him, promising he will never let us down. As a result, we revere him as our only King!

If we want to do great things for God, we must spend great time with him, so much so that when others look at us, they see him. Heaven forbid they walk away, having only seen us and only tasting what we have to give. Heaven forbid they walk away, starving for the Bread of Life. Our prayer should be that when our service is complete—when our hands are still and our voices are quiet—that those we served, though they might forget our faces, names, and what we did and said, they may always see, hear, and know Jesus.

To become godly leaders who feed Jesus' sheep with boldness, we must **appropriate Jesus, lead for Jesus, and bring Jesus to others.** *We will overcome the temporal and lead for eternity as we trust the eternal God.*

Questions for Discussion

1. What confusion or chaos do you need to overcome? Spiritually? Physically? Emotionally?

2. How is Jesus honing your vision as you've studied this book and taken a closer look at your leadership?

3. Describe the leadership struggles that tempt you toward independence.

4. What distracts you from beginning each day with Jesus? How might you overcome those distractions?

5. What, in your leadership, have you decided is too difficult for God?

6. What do you require that God is not providing?

7. How have you been tested in your leadership? What tool did you use to persevere?

8. Have you practiced praying with gratitude for what you have not yet or perhaps will not receive? How has that affected your perspective on whether or not you need it?

9. Describe your most significant area of poverty. How is Jesus using that area to prove his sufficiency?

10. What area of your leadership is the most difficult to surrender to Jesus? Why?

Afterword

Dear Friend,

You are a servant and you are a leader. It is the God of the universe who has called you to feed his sheep. I hope that this book has encouraged you to go wherever he has called you and do whatever he has asked of you.

This is my prayer for you as you accept his call and step out in faith:

Almighty, glorious, and holy God. We love you and desire more than anything to bring honor and glory to your name. Father, I lift up these, your servants, who are heeding your call to feed your sheep. I pray, God, that they will experience you in ways they never could have imagined as you undergird them and provide for them. Allow each to grow in spiritual maturity as they trust in you. As they apply these truths to their service, please show them your mighty hand of provision and perseverance. Father, I ask that you equip them for every good work and sustain them when things get difficult. Please give them the strength to seek you in the hard times and joy as they glorify you in the victories. I ask that many more souls will come to know you through their service and that heaven will be filled with satisfied sheep fed by the hands of these faithful ones.

In God's service,
Marcia

www.ingramcontent.com/pod-product-compliance
Lightning Source LLC
LaVergne TN
LVHW011935070526
838202LV00054B/4658